LEAVING THE CHURCH
TO *FIND GOD*

Moving from Spiritual Dissatisfaction to Spiritual Fulfillment

JOHN FENN

First published by Dog Ear Publishing
4010 W. 86th Street, Ste H
Indianapolis, IN 46268
www.dogearpublishing.net

ISBN: 978-159858-316-8

This book is printed on acid-free paper.

Printed in the United States of America

Introduction

God is moving on the planet on a scale that is unprecedented in history yet has been below the radar of the traditional churches. Christians are leaving the traditional church at an alarming rate across denominational and non-denominational lines, but for the first time in history they aren't dropping out to fall away from God, they are leaving to find God—to answer their spiritual dissatisfaction, their hunger for more of God.

You hear it in casual talk among church going friends; they aren't really happy in their spiritual life. The problem isn't really their church; it's just church in general. Expecting church to touch them deeply and desiring to be touched by God in a service, they are instead feeling the same when they leave as when they came in. They wonder if something is wrong with them and some even begin to doubt how much is real and how much is hype. But at the same time they feel it's something down inside them that is searching for something more. Deep inside there is a dissatisfaction they can't quite put their finger on.

Even if they have a church they call home, they find themselves keeping an eye open for guest speakers at other churches, and use that opportunity to sample other churches in town. If they don't have a church they call home, they attend wherever and whenever the urge hits them, they are what pastors call 'floaters'. Still others have just stopped going to church; they are de-churched.

Then I noticed a longing for something more welling up inside me, and I became one of those Christians who had told me they felt disconnected from church, though they were actively involved. Why did I feel disconnected? I was looking for the answers, but I never quite fit in, and eventually I wondered if there was a larger process at work in me. I started to realize I wasn't alone in my sense of searching for more in church. From all walks of life and across the church spectrum people are searching for something, but they don't quite know what.

The more I looked for God in the traditional church the more frustrated I became. I started wondering; are there other ways of doing church? I was searching for God and in times past I'd always sought Him within the confines of the traditional church structure, but the more I looked around it became clear that I had to look outside the traditional church to find God. This is the story of how I found God moving outside the church that I had known, loved, and been a part of my whole Christian life.

Table of Contents

Chapter 1

Divine Dissatisfaction

The man on the other end of the phone was a leader in the worship department at a large church in town. "I'm surrounded by people, but I'm lonely" he confessed. "You seem like a person I can talk to".

As we talked he explained that he felt wrapped up in the business of presenting a worship experience for the congregation, but didn't feel he was really touching God, nor being touched by God's Spirit. His relationships with the staff and volunteers of the church were shallow and church related only. There were no true friendships.

As I listened to his anguish—loving the church and it's vision but not feeling close to God or people in the church—I saw a reflection of my own heart. I had wondered if there was something wrong with me—Why was I yearning for more at church, feeling like I was on the outside looking in, surrounded by people but alone, and searching for a move of God?

After we had talked a number of times about our spiritual hunger and lack of fulfillment I became like a person considering the purchase of a certain model of car and now suddenly noticed all of those models on the road: Everywhere I turned I ran into people who expressed the same sense of yearning for something more that my new friend and I had.

Now I understood there were others who felt as I did. This realization was both comforting and scary, even confusing. I'd hear comments from others about how they had heard that same sermon several times before. Several came to me over the course of a few months asking why the order of service couldn't be thrown out the window just once so God could move freely. They expressed frustration when worship was really moving and God's presence could be felt, only to have it all cut off to receive the morning's offering.

Over the course of a couple months I made a point of speaking with several small group, or 'cell' leaders from various churches that were the most successful. Each confided that they did not follow the outline published in the church bulletin or other format for that week's lesson. They went with whatever the Lord seemed to want, and he touched people mightily in those groups. When I spoke with cell leaders that followed the bulletin published outline or prescribed lesson I found their groups struggled.

Was it a bad attitude to be disappointed with the Sunday sermon that week, no matter which church I was visiting at the time, realizing I'd heard that same message several times over the last few years in one form or another from a variety of pastors as I traveled in ministry? Was I just becoming bored with the routine of four songs, a 20 minute push for money, a video on one of the church outreaches and a 40 minute message? Was I so spiritually dense that I couldn't sense the Lord when the leaders said He was there? Was there something wrong with me? Or was it a matter of hype and crowd manipulation?

But when I scrutinized sermons there was no doubt I was seeing most of the messages and attitude of the churches geared towards money or "me" issues and not towards growing more Christ-like in character. Tired of messages about prosperity and faith on the one hand or the call for deliverance or salvation on the other; I needed practical messages on how to become more mature as a disciple of Jesus.

I then started hearing a lot of people describe themselves as being "between churches right now", when asked where they go to church. Like a person just fired but not wanting to say "I was fired," using the phrase "I'm between jobs right now," sounds so much nicer. It conveys that they are no longer employed where they were, yet they are actively looking.

Being "between churches" usually meant they were on good enough terms with their former church to attend if they so chose, but are visiting other churches until they find 'the right one'.

I became convinced that something was going on in the hearts of believers that could only be described as a divine dissatisfaction. It wasn't a matter of attitude, for like me, each person I encountered only wanted more of God, yet seemed increasingly frustrated at either the hype and money focus or the rigid and unresponsive structure that was their church home. It didn't matter if they were in the choir, cell group leader, Sunday school teacher, staff member, usher or not involved at all. All expressed the same spiritual dissatisfaction.

They were like someone having the 'thungries' about 8 or 9pm—Thungries are when you're not quite hungry but not just thirsty—you're thungry—You want something to eat but you don't know what it is. I met hundreds of Christians who knew they wanted something more, but didn't know how to get it or where to look. They had the spiritual 'thungries'. Like a person staring blankly at the opened refrigerator about 9pm and finding nothing that quite hits the spot, so too they were going from church to church not finding anything that satisfied.

When I searched down inside myself I realized I really just wanted a service where I could have an experience with God. Beyond that, I was searching for a dynamic faith that was connected to others on the same page. Rather than seeking the spectacular, I was looking for the supernatural, but every church I visited was just a slight variation on every other church I'd ever known.

When the church first started on the day of Pentecost it was a counterculture. They turned the world upside down with the message and changed people's lives for the better, changing the Roman Empire one house at a time over the span of 300 years until Christianity became legalized. But the church structure and culture I was in was a sub-culture not counterculture. We had our own dress, our own customs and our own language. I observed that in many churches the staff was dressed to the hilt while the congregation was dressed in jeans or other casual wear, yet the pastor and staff seemed totally unaware of how different they looked from the people they were supposedly ministering to.

One church staff member wrote a memo to the senior pastor suggesting dressing down for Wednesday night services (at least), and being careful to talk in terms that everyone could understand: What did it mean exactly for the pastor's wife to tell everyone the 'devil was after me all week, but when he showed up at my door I let him have it with the Word of God'? How was someone from outside the sub-culture of church supposed to understand what she said? Did the devil literally knock on her door and she threw a Bible at him?

He was later told that memo nearly got him fired, such was the entrenched mindset of the pastor; how dare anyone challenge the status quo!

Then came Julie (name changed for privacy). She was in her early 40s, single, active in the choir, took a couple classes at her church Bible school and was hungry for more of God. One morning someone called to tell me that she had driven to one of the lakes in the area the previous evening at sundown, put a loaded gun to her head and pulled the trigger.

I was shocked. How could a woman active in a large church, surrounded by a Bible school with about 200 students in her class, active in a choir of 200, commit suicide? How was it that she didn't have anyone to call, or worse yet, that none of us knew her well enough to call her?

How could God let her die like that? I was convinced that God's people in Julie's choir or Bible class would have reached out to her had they known she was struggling, so the problem was the way church was done that didn't promote relationships. No one knew her and she evidently didn't know a lot of people though she was active in church. I wondered what was wrong in the way we were doing church that such a person could slip between the cracks.

Rightly Dividing

I began to compare what I saw church had become with the way scripture said it should be. I had a basic understanding that Christianity was illegal or suffering persecution from Pentecost in about 32AD until the year 313AD, when Constantine issued the Edict of Milan, which legalized Christianity, making it the official religion of the Roman Empire. He then called people out of their homes and into the (former) pagan temples which used an auditorium style of seating.

It is this auditorium style that the gothic cathedrals were patterned after, and which all traditional churches are patterned after to this day, whether Protestant or Roman Catholic. Whether you sit in a pew in a denominational church or an arena style auditorium for church, the auditorium style seating began when Constantine called Christians out of their home based meetings and into the former pagan temples.

Noted author on cell churches Ralph Neighbour has stated that the clergy based part of the structure of the traditional church became further entrenched during a meeting of the bishops in 495AD, with the result being that only clergy would have the Word of God, and they would be responsible for telling the people what God was saying. The gift of pastor was elevated to become the single voice and leader over a church, but up until that time each house based church was led by the hosts and those elder in faith and life experience who were part of that church, in a mutually agreed upon direction.

Thus today the traditional church meets in a large auditorium patterned after a pagan temple with people gathering to hear one person designated as having the Word of the Lord for that meeting and every weekly meeting of that church.

That much was history and though different sources may list various dates for these events, the essential facts are well known. I wanted to be sure I wasn't going to be getting off balance in the way I was reading the New Testament when I compared the way church was being done today versus the way it was done in New Testament times.

I also realized some of their issues were unique to their time or culture; women wearing veils for instance, and I wanted to be sure I didn't carry a first century cultural issue forward into this century in my understanding of how to do church the New Testament way.

Jesus said in John 6:63;

"It is the Spirit that makes alive…the words that I speak to you, they are Spirit, and they are life". (KJV)

There must then be agreement between the Word and the Spirit in searching out any Biblical truth. The Spirit and the Word are in agreement.

For example, Peter was looking back at his experience on the Mount of Transfiguration as he wrote II Peter 1:16–21. During this experience he saw Moses and Elijah appear to a divinely illuminated Jesus and talk to him about his upcoming death in Jerusalem, and as a bright cloud enveloped them, he heard the Father speak. As Peter wrote this second letter he made the observation that as great as that vision and experience was,

"we have <u>a more sure word</u> of prophecy...knowing this first, that no prophecy (scripture) is of any private interpretation...but holy men of God spoke as they were moved by the Holy Spirit." (NKJV)

Thus he indicated that for any spiritual experience one may have, or if a person thinks God is moving in a particular way, it will be founded upon the scripture first, not the experience, for any spiritual experience must line up with the Word.

As great as his vision was of seeing Moses and Elijah speaking to a transfigured Jesus and hearing the Father God speak audibly, the Word of God is 'a more sure word', and therefore we must submit every experience to the scrutiny of scripture. Any experience or where and how we think God is moving will be supported by scripture. If it doesn't agree with the Word, it's not God, no matter how glorious the experience was. The Spirit and the Word will agree.

In Acts 15, about the year 51 AD, a great controversy arose about what if any of the laws of Moses should be imposed upon non-Jewish converts. Paul and Barnabus claimed God was moving among non-Jewish people, which was something outside the normal bounds of church, for up until then the church was almost exclusively Jewish and had been since the Day of Pentecost nearly 20 years earlier.

Now Paul and Barnabus claimed God was doing a new thing and it ruffled some feathers in the traditional church. One side said unless they were circumcised they couldn't be saved (Acts 15:1). The other side, which included Paul and Barnabus, said God's Spirit saved them and they didn't need to be circumcised and follow Moses' Laws.

Paul and Barnabus came before the leaders to see if they could continue with their practice of not requiring non-Jewish converts to obey the Law of Moses. James, the Lord's brother and now leader in Jerusalem listened intently to the debate. After a general discussion the first to speak was Peter (v6) who relayed his experience at Cornelius' house, the Roman Centurion (Acts 10). He told everyone how God poured out his Spirit upon that household and they all began speaking in tongues, an indication of God "knowing their hearts...purifying their hearts by faith" (v9). In speaking to the idea of requiring them to obey the Law of Moses, Peter asked; "…why tempt God, to put a yoke upon the neck of the disciples which neither our fathers nor we were able to bear?" (v10) Clearly Peter was siding with Paul and Barnabus.

The group next heard from Barnabus and Paul who declared "what miracles and wonders God had done among the Gentiles by them." (v12)

After hearing what the Holy Spirit had been doing among the Gentiles, James stood up and said,

> **"Peter has told you about the time God first visited the Gentiles to take from them a people to bring honor to His name. <u>And to this agree the words of the prophets: as it is written</u>…After this I will return…that the residue of men might seek after the Lord, and all the Gentiles, upon whom my name is called…" (Living Bible, 15:14–18) (Quoting Amos 9:11–12)**

In other words, James was listening to what Peter, Barnabus and Paul claimed God was doing among the Gentiles, and then found confirmation in the Word. In this way he could accurately determine if it was God or not, and once determined, he could take a course of action. In this case he saw that the Spirit and the Word agreed that God was indeed reaching out to non-Jews, and thus decided not to require the Gentiles to be circumcised, but only to refrain from idols, sexual sin and observe local Jewish dietary customs if there was a synagogue in the area (v19–21).

I began thinking about movements of God in my own time that started out as truly being from God, yet had gotten off balance and needed a council similar to Acts 15 so someone in authority could tell them they were in God's will or maybe had become off balanced.

Years ago what became known as the Shepherding movement brought many into accountability in the discipleship process. One could look in the Word and see strong relationships between Jesus and his disciples, Barnabus and Paul, Paul and Timothy, and even how Aquila and Priscilla got to know Apollos and "expounded the way of God more accurately to him." (Acts 18:26) A person can certainly see strong mentor/disciple relationships in the Word, thus we could conclude the Spirit was truly moving.

However, soon reports from the Shepherding movement began coming in that people in churches couldn't change jobs, buy cars or houses, or make other important decisions without first getting approval from their mentors or church elders. This kind of strict legalism is not found in the Word, and many declared these practices NOT to be God, and rightly so. The Word and the Spirit will agree and there is no place in the scripture such bondage is advocated; therefore a person could rightly divide where that movement crossed the line into error.

If a movement or message is about the Spirit only it will be flaky. If a movement or message is about the Word only it will be as dry as toast. There must be a balance between the Spirit and the Word in all things, and it is this balance I was seeking.

The Search Begins

Now armed with the understanding of how to search the Spirit and Word to discover what God might be doing, I began following the same pattern the apostle James followed in Acts 15, researching what if anything God was doing outside the traditional church. I began looking for modern day reports of God moving among people. If God's Spirit seemed to be moving out there in the world somewhere, then I would find it in the Word. If it couldn't be found in the Word it would be rejected and I'd keep looking.

I learned that Christianity is the fastest growing religion on earth, growing at about 8% per year (US Center for World Mission—uscwm.org & 'Megashift', Jim Rutz pgs15 & 44), and that this growth was almost exclusively in house based churches, the majority charismatic in nature. In fact, I learned the traditional church is losing members, even the evangelical and charismatic ones, or at the most barely treading water in terms of numbers while house based churches are part of an explosion of Christianity. In my travels I'd casually question pastors in various cities and often found that churches that were growing were actually just attracting people from other churches rather than adding disciples by getting people born again.

With only the slightest effort at keeping my eyes and ears open to what was happening in other countries, I learned that China's Christian population in particular was exploding. I heard and read people putting the numbers of Christians in China, all in house churches, between 120 million and 200 million.

Then I started hearing from people who were traveling the world in short and long-term missionary efforts. Their reports of house churches in Indonesia, India, Africa, Latin America, and the Arab world stirred my heart and confirmed the Spirit of God was moving outside the bounds of the traditional church I knew. People were leaving church to become the church, and I was hungry to hear more.

One lady reported on her 3 week stay in Indonesia: "I taught every day for several hours in the Bible school. Most of the students were new converts, but all of them were intent on starting churches in houses in all their villages and towns. And the amazing thing is that they mature very quickly and become leaders, maybe because of the persecution, maybe because of the nature of house churches, but within about 90 days a person goes from born again to church planter and leader."

I had lunch with a Malaysian man who started a Bible school in his own country. He told me the message he gets the greatest reaction from when preaching to people who don't know about Jesus, is the story of Jesus being betrayed at dinner by Judas in John 13. He said that people literally have tears streaming down their faces at the thought that someone at dinner had betrayed Jesus. This man explained that in oriental culture, and the Bible and Israel are oriental, having a meal with someone at home is the most intimate means of fellowship. He explained that in the orient, culture is all about the home, the village, and family. This realization helped explain the explosive growth of house churches in China, India and SE Asia; they're all relationship based.

A friend spent 3 weeks in China, meeting with Christians every day. She said they met in homes, the backs of restaurants, in courtyards found by walking down narrow alleys, and other places all in small groups, amongst families and villages.

It seemed that the revival US Christians had been praying for was well underway in the rest of the world, but because it was based in homes, families and villages rather than in the traditionally styled church it was under the radar of the US church world. I'd hear pastors and TV preachers call for revival, being completely blind to what is happening all over the world. Clearly they were looking for revival to come within their set of parameters, their traditional church structure.

Church leaders in America and Europe have been looking for revival, thinking revival meant hundreds or thousands of people flocking to their services, not realizing God was empowering millions to 'have church' in their own living rooms, huts, and businesses. People were learning to be the church instead of going to church, all without help from the traditional church.

God is de-centralizing the nations

When I took a step back from just focusing on the revival through house based churches around the world and started looking at the big picture that was happening in other segments of society, I realized something larger is going on.

Being a student of history I'd long been fascinated by the apparent link between the freedom of God's Word and Spirit in a society and the creativity and vitality of that society. By contrast I'd noticed the opposite was true—when God's Word and Spirit were not present or not allowed to move, societies were oppressive and had little creativity.

For instance, it seems more than coincidence that when the Word of God was locked away in monasteries and reserved only for clergy, Europe plunged into the

Dark Ages. By the same token, proportional to the degree God's Word was released into the hands of people through the King James and other translations of the Bible in the common language of the peoples of Europe; is when the Renaissance and Industrial Revolution began.

Early Bibles like The Wycliffe Version in about 1400 and The Tyndale Version 140 years later were matched by Gutenberg's printing press and the first ever mechanically printed Bible in 1456. For the first time God's Word was being printed in large numbers in the common language of a nation, rather than hand written in Latin for use only by clergy. Finally, in 1611 the King James Bible was printed in England, which led to the Bible's translation into other languages of Europe, and suddenly whole nations of people could understand God's Word. In this time frame the Industrial Revolution began.

We have only to look as far as the oppression of the Iron Curtain and lack of creativity within the USSR as an example in our own times of the relationship between the freedoms of God's Word versus the Word locked away. While the US and west were exploding with creativity and progress following the end of WW II, the USSR was stagnant. While staying with some new Russian friends in Yekaterinburg shortly after the wall came down, our hostess said: "For 70 years we were told our society was the most modern and prosperous, and in one day we discovered it was a lie. Our society had not changed since WW II while the rest of world had."

It's no coincidence that China's exploding economy and experimentation with capitalism in our time is happening at the same time the greatest revival in the world is happening through house church there.

Following WW II, in the west starting in 1947, God poured out his Spirit in a great healing movement that continued into the 1960s. Names like Kathryn Kuhlman, Oral Roberts, Jack Coe, AA Allen and many others brought the revelation that God heals people to millions. Billy Graham's ministry rose up during this time and millions came to the Lord. Oral Roberts went on TV, bringing his healing crusades to the masses.

As the healing movement waned in the late 1960s the Charismatic Renewal exploded on the scene. Many translations and paraphrases of the Bible were coming from publishers in easily read and studied formats, and Christian bookstores began popping up all over the country to help put products into the common people's hands. This had the effect of empowering the individual in Christ in their own private time with God, whereas before a person depended on that once a week feeding from their Seminary trained pastor on Sunday morning for their spiritual sustenance. In direct correlation to these moves of God technology in the United States was taking off. As Christians were being empowered in their faith, technology was also empowering individuals, causing a de-centralization of many time honored institutions as it was also rocking the traditional church structure.

When I was growing up, if a musician wanted to make a record, they had to get a contract with one of the few recording studios—Motown in Detroit, Capital Records in LA, or maybe in Memphis or Nashville. As technology has empowered the individual, now any musician with a computer, recordable CD and some sound equipment can make their own album, AND put it on the Internet for millions to hear, all from the comfort of their living room. Lawsuits between the music and movie industries and internet based web sites demonstrate the battle between the institution and individual rights.

In the same way, Education has become decentralized. Computer based classes and web-casts now enable people pursuing their degree to attend classes while seated at their home computer. Some graduate from a college without ever having set foot on the central campus. Related to education is the concept of the library. No longer does a person have to go downtown to the city library or to a main college campus, for with a few clicks on the computer the knowledge of the world is sent directly to your fingertips.

Perhaps the leading edge of individual empowerment in education in the 1980s was the home schooling movement. When our children were little and we home schooled in the 1980s, home schooling was still struggling for acceptance, banned in some states unless the parent teaching the child was a state certified teacher, and outright illegal in still others. The public schools and the general public's mood in general were not favorable towards home schooling, yet the empowerment of the individual marched on. Twenty five years later, today in the US home schooling has gained acceptance and is excelling.

The health care industry used to be centralized around the big city hospital, which was a one stop shop for health care. Today same-day surgery clinics are all over, and there are specialty hospitals—one for spines, another for hearts, one for eyes, and even birthing centers—all specialized for just one discipline.

Perhaps the biggest battle between individual freedoms and the power of a centralized institution in the US is fought in the halls of Congress. Issues like Universal Health Care, Social Security, entitlement programs, and a host of other issues are basically about empowering either the government or the individual. It's a battle of big government socialism or individual freedoms. The reason the topic is so hot now is because on a scale much larger than merely the US government, God is moving in all areas to empower individuals, first to know Him and become a disciple of Jesus, and then overflowing to the rest of a culture and society.

Whenever God moves on the planet, he affects society as a whole, even if they don't realize it. In the same way that industry, education, health care, entertainment (and a host of other segments of society) are being decentralized, so is the traditional church. God is focusing on the empowerment of individuals in their walk with him, and the traditional church, like other institutions in society, is feeling the effects. The power of individual empowerment unleashed on the earth in secular institutions is actually just a by-product of God moving among his people all over the planet.

God the Father can't help but give life and light and creativity when he starts in a certain direction in the same way Jesus couldn't help but to bring life and healing wherever he went. But today through the Spirit, He is moving all over the planet. The world thinks technology is driving the empowerment of the individual, but in reality it is the Spirit of God being poured out in the earth in His people.

Between 313 AD when people came out of their homes and into former pagan temples to have church, up until the Charismatic Movement of the 1960s and 70s there was largely only 1 way to do church, and the only way to learn about God was through the seminary trained Reverend who told you each Sunday morning what God said. But when God's Word started getting into the hands of the common people in translations they could understand and relate to in the 1960s and 70s, with all the accompanying study helps, worship music, and daily devotionals for them to use, the ability of those individuals to hear from God for themselves opened up a brave new world. People no longer had to depend on their pastor alone to tell them what God was saying; they could hear from God for themselves!

The progression of this means people are less and less loyal to one congregation, they will now go where they can get fed, and if they can't find a suitable church, they can stay home and have church themselves.

Ramifications of Empowerment

It should be noted however that individual empowerment without discipline is anarchy, a state in which no one rules, there is no order, and confusion reigns. However, because the Christian knows they are accountable to God and to their fellow man, there should not be a case of a Christian being totally on his own, his own Master, an island.

As I was searching this out I began searching for God's answer to balance the way he was empowering people. I had run across too many people saying "I answer only to Jesus", which to them meant they were a part of no one, no one spoke into their lives, and their statement was a bluff and façade meant to keep people at bay while they did their own thing without any accountability.

I also saw people who had no business leading a home based church or prayer and praise meeting doing so, with the results being spiritually hurt and injured Christians. Where was the balance?

When looking in the Word I saw that people were accountable to each other. Even Peter, Paul, and Barnabus were willing to go to Jerusalem and submit their lives to the scrutiny of their peers. The churches Paul started or had a hand in were connected both to him and each other, regularly receiving visitors from other churches and even sending offerings to Paul and/or Jerusalem and other places. The Apostle John wrote The Revelation to the 7 churches of Asia, but it wasn't John who had started those churches, it was Paul and his converts, yet they willingly received John's ministry. Everyone was connected to everyone else, thus through mutual accountability the whole of Christianity grew in a balanced fashion, at a pace corresponding to the quality of the relationships.

In His empowerment of the individual, God balanced freedom by requiring us to walk out that freedom in relationships which are transparent, honest, and close. Righteousness most certainly comes through knowing Christ, yet it's unproven if it remains solely in the heart of a person. Righteousness must therefore be lived within a framework of relationships, thus maturing us as we walk through life together, iron sharpening iron, speaking into each other's lives; developing long and enduring friendships.

By contrast I was seeing all around me Christians with no one close to them, accountable to no one whether they were in a church, started their own home based church, or had become de-churched and dropped out altogether. Some started home groups that were nothing more than either bless me clubs or private miniature pulpits for frustrated preachers who had an axe to grind. A recent study mentioned on the evening news said 25% of all people have not a single friend. And the average of those who do have friends is down 1 friend compared to 10 years ago. This is not God's way, for freedom means free to become involved in each other's lives, not the freedom to become an island to oneself.

No matter the institution, when the individual is empowered people either drop out of the institutions or they stay and try to change them from within. Therefore bureaucracies and institutions fall or decentralize for if they don't adapt they become antiquated and irrelevant to the people; and this is what I was seeing happen in the traditional church. The centralized institution (and its' leaders) begin losing influence as the individual is empowered, and the individual becomes personally responsible in whatever area they are now empowered.

To answer the needs for individual empowerment I saw churches delegate authority to some members by trying various forms of small groups, with some success, but many others going through program after program trying to instill life into their congregation and develop relationships with little success.

I realized that the reason I was bored with the sermons I was hearing was that I was able to have more depth in my own studies than what the pastors seemed able to muster. As I talked to people who attended successful small groups in various churches I heard repeatedly that they got their nourishment from the small group, and not from Sunday morning's sermon and service. Many told me they didn't even go to Sunday morning services, but only to the small group.

This raised all sorts of conflicts within me: Pastors were supposed to be more mature than their congregation, deeper spiritually, yet their messages were entirely too shallow. It was in the small groups of many churches that I found life, yet the groups where God was moving didn't follow the published outline. How was it God was moving in living rooms but not in the Sunday service? Was something wrong with me, all these people, the pastor, or the structure? People were asking themselves whether they wanted to attend a church where they had more depth than the pastor. They found it hard justifying the giving of hard earned money to someone that was becoming more and more irrelevant to their life.

God's empowerment of the individual which was ordained to be Life was causing me and many others to take personal responsibility for our own spirituality in ways heretofore not experienced. Up until this point I was happy enough going to church because it was the thing to do and because I got something out of it. There was a balance between my personal devotion time and Sunday morning. But now Sunday morning didn't do anything for me so I was being forced to deal with an ever-growing dissatisfaction within, and so were people all around me.

As I looked for God, I found Him more in His people than I did in His structure of church, and that was a realization that shocked me. The busy-ness of church was actually harming the very institutions of marriage, family, and relationships it purported to support. By requiring people to be at church every time the doors were opened, families were going their separate ways once through those doors—the baby to the nursery, the youngsters to children's church, the teens to youth group, and the parents to the main service—all having separate experiences within the structure, not as a family experiencing God. This practice leaves families feeling disconnected from each other as it delegates the job of teaching children about God to strangers. From there the disconnected feeling grows to church and then God in general.

It was like each church I visited had a group of people within the church looking for more, yet afraid to talk about it lest they be labeled as having an attitude. They knew it wasn't a matter of attitude, yet many who had been brave enough to bring up issues to church leaders were accused of having a bad attitude. In truth, they just wanted God to be able to have his way in a service and be connected to their families and friends instead of following the set formula each week.

Like the little boy in "The Emperor's New Clothes" who spoke honestly that the Emperor was naked, so too I wanted to stand up and tell the leadership they and their structure were irrelevant and boring me and I was tired of having the pastoral cheerleaders entertain and manipulate me! I wanted them to let go and let God flow!

Too many were just dropping out, stopping their church attendance altogether and I didn't want to join their ranks—the Word says not to forsake the gathering together of ourselves. However, for every person I found that just dropped out of church and wasn't going anywhere, I found many more that were having meetings with friends during a weeknight, similar to the "prayer and praise" meetings I attended as a teenager in the 1970s.

The Question

Thus the question became one of what was I going to do with this empowerment and freedom? Was my deep yearning within to seek spiritual fulfillment and do church differently stronger than the ingrained church culture I'd known all my life? Was I one to hunker down and plod mindlessly into church each Sunday morning the rest of my life, or would I be willing to look elsewhere, even if that was outside the only way I knew of doing church?

The empowerment of the individual to seek and learn about Christ is the single greatest factor that enables a person to become a disciple of Jesus. Our life in Christ and our growth in Him are in our own hands and always have been. When I was first born again it was an individual, a friend who brought me to Christ. I then learned and grew through other newly found friends in the midst of informal Thursday night, Saturday night, and Sunday night "prayer and praise" meetings. Sunday morning services did little for me; my growth was spurred on by close friends who helped answer questions and guide me into maturity in Christ.

When I looked at the reports of the apparent explosion of house based churches around the world, and compared that freedom and empowerment to the traditional church structure, plus added in what was happening in societies around the world through individual empowerment, I knew God was marching on the planet in ways that were affecting whole nations. God seemed to be empowering people in every walk of life and segment of society, but could I find it in the Bible?

Home is for learning about God

When I looked at the big picture and saw the Spirit of God moving in the homes, villages and cultures all over the world on an individual rather than institutional basis, I had to find the root of it all. Realizing that the traditionally structured church of today actually began following the 313AD Edict of Milan made me realize that church as I knew it is a man made invention, not God made. For the first (nearly) 300 years of Christianity, the church met in homes exclusively. It was this format that turned the Roman Empire upside down in spite of intense persecution, through a groundswell rising from living rooms all over the Empire. I could see the house church movement in China changing it in the midst of persecution in our own day and age as well. Surely there was something to this.

Yet the argument could be made that Constantine's idea was a God-idea; that it was time for people to come out of homes and into the auditorium and clergy structure we know today. Perhaps the house-based first 300 years of Christianity had matured to the point that meeting in homes was no longer relevant and a change was needed, and God met that need through Constantine's legalization of the faith.

God works in order, line upon line; precept upon precept, so if house based church was the foundation laid at the day of Pentecost and Constantine's structure of today's traditional church was the next level built upon that foundation, I wondered if there was a stronger foundation that undergirds both ways of doing church?

The Big Question about house based churches

The question I was asking was; Are there eternal, essential qualities in a home setting that remain untouched by the hands of time and can't be duplicated outside the home? Or are those in house based church trying to go back to a first century format to resurrect something from which time and culture have moved on?

Are there eternal, essential qualities in a home setting that remain untouched by the hands of time and can't be duplicated outside the home?

Actually, I discovered it's much more than that! The precedent of church in the house goes all the way back to Adam and Eve. You may recall that the Lord planted a garden for Adam and Eve which was their home, and he walked with them in the midst of it. Based on Jesus' later statement that "where two or three are gathered together in my name, there am I in the midst of them" (Mt 18:20) the first home based church was the Garden of Eden. It was in this home that the Lord instructed Adam about the trees. It was in this home Adam received direction from the Lord to cultivate the Garden and named the animals. It was also in this home Eve was formed from Adam's body, having the Lord himself bring her to him (Gen 2:22).

As time went on God's emphasis on the home continued to be revealed. In Genesis 18:1–20 the Lord and two angels appear to Abraham in human form, and have dinner with him. After dinner the Lord rises to make his way towards Sodom (v16), and he says to himself:

"Shall I hide from Abraham that thing which I do...For I know him, that he will command his children and his household after him, and they shall keep the way of the Lord..." (KJV)

Here we see a case of the Lord about to bring judgment on Sodom and Gomorrah but he did not withhold that information from Abraham because he knew his home was a place where the Lord and His ways lived. To say it another way, God was inclined to share His plans with Abraham because Abraham lived the ways of God in his home, before his wife and children. It was the quality of Godly family life that Abraham had that caused the Lord to pause and share His plans about Sodom and Gomorrah with him.

The Lord didn't reveal his plans to Abraham out in the wilderness during a time of sacrificial worship, but rather in his home, just after a meal.

When we look at the 10 Commandments (Ex 20: 1–17), it is widely observed that the first 4 commandments have to do with man's worship of God. (You will have no other gods, shall not make a graven image, God's name is sacred, honor the Sabbath) Commandment #1 summarizes the other 3, and they derive their strength from that first command.

Similarly commandment number 5 summarizes the rest of the commandments which all have to do with how man treats man. What is that 5th commandment? "Honor your father and your mother". All the rest of the commandments—don't murder, don't commit adultery, don't steal, don't lie, don't covet—are all built around the father and mother imparting these truths to their children and household. This is why the summary of the commandments is to love the Lord with all your heart, soul, and mind, and love your neighbor as yourself—the essence of Commandments 1 and 5. (Mark 12:29–31)

It should come as no surprise then to learn that the whole of Jewish culture places high emphasis on learning from one's elders, the family unit, and a style of learning that revolves around walking through life <u>with</u> a person as they apply God's Word into their lives.

Besides the Lord's observation about Abraham instructing his household in the ways of God, the instructions of Deuteronomy 4:4–9 stand out:

"Hear O Israel: The Lord our God is one Lord...and these words shall be in your heart...and you shall teach them diligently to your children, and shall talk of them when you sit in your house, and when you walk by the way, and when you lie down, and when you rise up..." (KJV)

Even Solomon, in the book of Proverbs, claims to be only repeating what his father David taught him from 4:4 through the end of chapter 9. Consider Proverbs 4:3–7:

"For I was my father's (David) son, tender and only beloved in the sight of my mother (Bathsheba), He taught me and said to me, "Let your heart retain my words, keep my commandments and live. Get wisdom and understanding…wisdom is the principle thing, therefore get wisdom…" (KJV)

Is it any wonder that when the Lord appeared to Solomon and said: "Ask what I shall give you", that Solomon responded:

"Give me now wisdom and knowledge…" (II Chron 1:7, 10) (KJV)

Solomon asked for wisdom because David and Bathsheba, in their home, had instructed him to seek wisdom as he was growing up!

The whole of Proverbs 4 through 9 are Solomon quoting his father David beginning with "He taught me and said to me…" and through chapter 9 Solomon quotes his father David. Chapter 10:1 transitions from quoting his dad to his own words: "The Proverbs of Solomon. A wise son makes a glad father: but a foolish son is the heaviness of his mother…"

The book of Judges records that one of Israel's first rulers, Deborah, was "a mother in Israel" as she settled disputes and ruled the land (Ju 5:7). Elijah's students in his school of the prophets were called 'the sons of the prophets' (II Kings 2:3). Another example is when Elijah was taken away by the fiery chariot and his assistant and successor, Elisha, called out: "My father! My father!" (II Kings 2:11–12). And of course Malachi, the last book of the Old Testament, in the last line of that book, says the coming work of the Lord will be to turn the hearts of the fathers to the children, and the heart of the children to their fathers. (Mal 4:6)

I came to understand that from the Garden of Eden throughout the Old Testament, God had made the determination that the home would be the central place for learning about God. I also realized that heaven, our eternal destination, is God's home, the place Jesus went to prepare for us so that one day we could live with him there! God started mankind off by meeting him in the home he had prepared for him, and we will end up in God's home as well!

Now I understood the basis for having church in the home. It was not just a New Testament phenomenon of people forced into homes by a non-responsive Jewish culture and Roman occupation, the home was God's choice for learning about

Him from the start. God had ordained the home and family as the central place to meet God and learn of Him long before New Testament times!

Learning about God in the home was a previous and greater foundation for church and was in place long before the day of Pentecost. When the church age began on Pentecost meeting in the homes was the obvious and natural extension of the learning that was already taking place there. In fact, it was this emphasis on home that allowed Jesus to come into this world, growing up in a family and tight knit community.

In my search for God, if I did leave the traditional church to find Him, this meant I was merely returning home, where my wife and I had always focused on the Lord with our three sons and close friends. In times past I'd searched for the Lord in the structure of the traditional church, but I was beginning to see the Lord in His people in a sense of community with those on the same spiritual page, and there was something that resonated in me that this was a deeper truth than the church structure I'd known all my life.

Constantine's calling the Christians out of the homes into legalized religion was man's idea, not God's. Furthermore, God has never stopped using the home and families as the central place for spreading the knowledge and ways of the Lord. However, God's moving in individual empowerment all over the world has gathered so much momentum that the traditional church is being shaken by all those coming out of her, leaving to go home and the close relationships of family and friends to learn of God!

Once I started to see traditional church for what it was, a rather recent invention, not the original plan, I realized my mind was programmed by this design of man. As a result, I wanted to see the scripture anew, as if I wasn't programmed by a life time of looking at scripture through the traditional structure of church. I worked to remove all assumptions about what church was, stripping away the layers of thoughts and concepts, comparing each of my beliefs with what scripture actually said on the subject of how church was to be conducted, and even the very definition of church.

I began to look for continuity in the Gospels and rest of the New Testament. Consider that Jesus' first miracle of turning water into wine was in a house (John 1:11); Jesus taught and healed in homes—including Peter's mother-in law (Mk 1:29–30); Jesus was anointed for his burial at the end of a meal in Lazarus' home (John 12:1–8); the Last Supper was in a home (John 22:11); Pentecost took place in a home (Acts 2:2); and so on. When we walk through the book of Acts we see Dorcas raised from the dead in a house (9:36–43), the apostles and later Paul teaching in houses, Cornelius' household saved in a house (10:30, 44)…and the list goes on. Why? Because the home is where instruction and the application of that instruction took place! The home is the central place of learning and doing, and has been since the Lord met with Adam and Eve in the Garden of Eden.

God's Moving Day

When the day of Pentecost came and "filled the house where they were sitting" the church age began. Spilling into the streets, Peter delivered a message that resulted in about 3,000 converts made up at least in part by visitors in town for the feast (2:41). Peter stated this outpouring of God's Spirit was the fulfillment of a prophecy of Joel 2:28–32, that indicates the following would be characteristics of this move of God: The Holy Spirit was poured out on men and women of all ages, and included prophecy, visions, spiritual dreams, signs and wonders, and salvation for those who would believe. This event marked the beginning of the 'last days' (2:17).

I want to emphasize the impact of Peter's message. His hearers were visitors from all over the Roman Empire—modern day Iran, Iraq, Turkey, Egypt, Libya, Rome, Crete, various Arab countries and more are mentioned. They had come to Jerusalem to worship at the temple for the feast of Pentecost.

Peter's statement that God was pouring out his Spirit on ALL flesh meant the temple and the temple priests were no longer THE place to find God's presence, but that each individual had God in him or her by believing on and receiving Jesus as Lord!

Sadly, we have been raised in the traditional church to first think of God's presence filling 'the house of the Lord' rather than us. I remember being about 8 years old when my mom brought me in the back of St. Andrews Episcopal Church in Kokomo, Indiana for the first time. I started talking out loud, asking questions, and my mom quieted me saying, "Shh, we need to be quiet, this is God's house".

I remember being amazed and asking where he was. She directed my attention to a lamp burning near the altar, saying that flame represents God's presence. I was confused and thinking that if God was in that flame I could go up there and blow it out; what did she mean? Fortunately she told me the flame represents the presence of God being in the church and not God Himself, but for years afterward I always checked that flame to make sure it was still lit when I came to a service.

I developed a respect for the things of God, and eventually, following my mom's lead, was born again as a teenager so I am very thankful for that upbringing, however, God doesn't live in the building; he lives in the people who come to the building.

If Peter was saying that God's Spirit was now being poured out on individuals instead of in the temple in Jerusalem, how and why did God get into the temple in the first place, and why the change?

After Israel comes out of Egypt and makes its' way to Mt. Sinai, Exodus 19:3–20 records the Lord coming out of the unseen spiritual realm to meet personally with Moses on top of the mountain. He told Moses that they were called out of Egypt so they could become <u>a kingdom of priests to the Lord</u> (19:6), and the Lord instructed Moses to make a place where God could live among his people, called the tabernacle. In 25:21–22 he tells Moses to make a gold-covered box with two gold-covered cherubs stretching over it,

> **"...and there I will meet with you, and I will commune with you from above the mercy seat, from between the two cherubim which are on the ark of the testimony..." (KJV)**

Understand what happened. God called Israel out of Egypt to meet with him at Mt. Sinai, telling them they were to be a kingdom of priests. But in 20:18–21 the people rejected their priesthood and asked the Lord to talk only to Moses and let him tell them what he said.

> **"And they said to Moses, You speak with us, and we will listen, but don't let God speak with us lest we die...and the people moved far off, but Moses drew near to the cloud where God was." (KJV)**

God had called them out of Egypt to meet with him, and now he was telling Moses to make him a home so that he could live among the people. But because they rejected their own priesthood and wanted Moses to tell them what God had said, the Lord accepted that, appointing Moses' family, the Levites, to stand in the people's stead. That is how the priests of Levi were formed, after the people rejected being the kingdom of priests which was God's original intention.

The temple mentality of Israel who rejected their own priesthood remains in most Christian's minds today in the traditionally structured Sunday morning service. The mind-set that one person heading up a temple style service will communicate God's Word to 'non-clergy' started when the people told Moses they'd prefer he just told them what God was saying, rather than them being personally involved in hearing from God for themselves.

The Levitical priesthood operated around the tabernacle and temple in much the same way people in the pews today are mere bystanders, as designated worshippers and clergy conduct a Sunday morning service.

God still got his way however, and that is exactly what Peter was saying on the day of Pentecost. By moving out of the temple and into individuals who wanted him living inside them, God had made for himself a kingdom of priests. That is why Revelation 1:6 and 5:10 each declare that we are now 'a kingdom of priests unto God'.

Let us return to the progression of events. God called Israel out of Egypt to meet with him at the mountain. There he instructed Moses to build a tent and Ark of the Covenant where God could live and be with his people. But, after the golden calf incident the Lord told Moses in Exodus 33:3–11 that he had better move him out of the camp lest he destroy the whole nation (NKJV):

> **"...I will not go up in the middle of you; for you are a rebellious people...And Moses took the tabernacle and pitched it outside the camp, far off from the camp...And it came to pass that everyone who sought the Lord went out to the tabernacle that was (now) outside the camp. And it came to pass as Moses entered into the tabernacle the cloudy pillar descended (from off the mountain), and stood at the door of the tabernacle, and the Lord talked with Moses. And all the people saw the cloudy pillar stand at the tabernacle door, and they rose up to worship, every man at his tent door. And the Lord spoke to Moses face to face, as a man speaks to his friend..."**

The Lord was faithful to live in the tabernacle outside the camp, traveling with Israel through the 40 years of wandering in the wilderness. As Numbers 9:15–23 records, the people pitched camp when the cloudy pillar stopped, and they packed up and moved when the pillar of God's presence moved.

> **"...whether it was two days, or a month, or a year, that the cloud stayed above the tabernacle, the children of Israel stayed in their tents and didn't travel: but when it was taken up, they traveled." (KJV)**

Eventually Israel crossed the Jordan into the Promised Land, always protecting the Ark of the Covenant and God's manifest presence down through the years. Once David is made king some 400 years after Moses' first meeting God at the mountain, one of his first acts is to bring the Ark of the Covenant to Jerusalem. He knows God as the "one who lives between the cherubs". II Samuel 6:2

"...and David went with all the people...to bring up the ark of God, whose name is called by the name of <u>the Lord of hosts who lives between the cherubs</u>". (NKJV)

Though Moses, Joshua, and the Judges have come and gone, in David's time God is still living between the cherubs on the gold-covered box that Moses built.

In II Samuel 7:2 David comes to a startling revelation; he lives in a palace built of stone and cedar, but God still lives in a tent! He wants to make a house for the Lord and tells Nathan the prophet:

"...See now, I live in a house of cedar, but the ark of God lives in a cloth tent...(v4) and it came to pass that night the Word of the Lord came to Nathan saying, Go tell my servant David, Do you want to build me a house to live in? <u>I have not lived in any house since the time that I brought up the children of Israel out of Egypt, even to this day, but have lived in a tent and in a tabernacle</u>. In all the places I have walked with all the children of Israel did I speak a word at any time to the tribes of Israel, 'Why don't you build me a house of cedar?'...when your days are fulfilled you will sleep with your fathers, I will set up your seed after you...and I will establish his kingdom (Solomon). He will build a house for my name and I will establish the throne of his kingdom forever." (NKJV)

Solomon did take the throne after David's death and he built the temple in about 960BC. For years we've marveled at the presence of God poured out during the dedication of Solomon's temple, but have failed to realize this 'moving day' for God was just part of the succession of events that began with God meeting Moses in a thick dark cloud on Mt. Sinai some 440 years earlier. The pillar that came off the mountain to enter the tabernacle is the same pillar that entered the Temple of Solomon with the ark, as described in II Chronicles 5:7, 13–14.

"And the priests brought the ark of the covenant of the Lord to his place...to the most holy place, even under the wings of the cherubim...then the house was filled with a cloud, even the house of the Lord; so that the priests could not stand (up) to minister because of the cloud: for the glory of the Lord had filled the house of God". (KJV)

Solomon also says in 6:2

"The Lord has said that he would live in thick darkness (see Ex 19:16) but I have built a house for you, and a place for you to live in forever." (NKJV)

And this is where God lived from the time of Solomon until the day of Pentecost.

Though Solomon's original temple was destroyed, then rebuilt in about 500BC, then remodeled and added to by Herod shortly before Jesus came, God always moved into the temple in Jerusalem, manifesting his presence between the cherubs. That is where you could find him, and that is why all those people from all over the Roman Empire were in Jerusalem during the Day of Pentecost.

On the day of Pentecost God moved out of the temple and from between the cherubim, and into the recreated spirits of people who would receive him, some 120 at first then another 3,000.

Peter eloquently quoted Joel when he said that God is pouring out his Spirit on all flesh of all ages and gender, but Paul put it more bluntly in Acts 17 during his message to the idol worshippers on Mars Hill, Athens:

"God who has made the world and everything in it, seeing that he is Lord of heaven and earth, <u>does not live in a temple made with hands.</u>" (Acts 17:24—KJV)

It is interesting that Paul first heard that phrase from Steven, during his last words before he was martyred and to which Paul was present in Acts 7: 48:

"However the Most High does not dwell in houses and temples made with hands..." (AMP)

Neither Steven nor Paul could have made those statements before the day of Pentecost; for up until that time God lived exclusively in the temple in Jerusalem. But the Day of Pentecost had arrived and God had moved out of the temple and into people. Paul would later write:

"Do you not discern and understand that you (the whole church at Corinth) are God's temple, and that God's Spirit has His permanent dwelling in you (to be at home in you, collectively as a church and also individually?)" (I Cor 3:16 AMP)

"Do you not know that your body is the temple (the very sanctuary) of the Holy Spirit Who lives within you?" (I Cor 6:19) (NKJV)

And:

"We have this treasure in earthen vessels that the excellency of the power may be of God, and not of us." (II Cor 4:7—KJV)

Peter, Paul and the apostles understood that individuals, together as the whole of the body of Christ, now make up the temple of God:

"...and the cornerstone of the building is Jesus Christ himself! We who believe are carefully joined together with Christ as parts of a beautiful, constantly growing temple for God. And you also are joined with him and with each other by the Spirit, and are part of this dwelling place of God." (Eph 2:20–22 Living)

"Come to Christ, who is the living foundation of Rock upon which God builds...and now you have become living building-stones for God's use in building his house: What's more, you are His holy priests..." (I Peter 2:4–5 Living)

So now, instead of one temple in Jerusalem, God had moved, and moves today, into anyone one who wants to be his temple. In this way it is much more efficient, and as Jesus said, better that he went away. By entering into individuals, God could take his message and presence all over the earth, allowing each person to be used by him according to their own gifts and call in life. Jesus as the head of the church oversees and orchestrates from heaven how his body moves on the earth.

The Genesis Command

The Master Plan of God actually follows his command in Genesis to his creation. "Be fruitful and multiply, fill the earth". (Gen 1:28/9:1) It should come as no surprise that God obeys his own commands, and he has tried to fill the earth from the beginning. Ephesians 1:23, speaking of Jesus states:

"...who fills everything everywhere with Himself." (AMP)

Christ Jesus, by entering into people as temples through the Holy Spirit, is Himself seeking to fulfill the Genesis command to fill the earth. <u>From His effort to fill the earth by filling all individuals flow all the moves of God we have ever seen, or ever will see on the earth.</u> And like his creation, he adapts to whatever structure man gives him.

When Paul told the people on Mars Hill that God didn't live in a temple but in people, he was talking about this Genesis command to fill the earth in Acts 17: 26–28:

> **"He created all the people of the world from one man, Adam, and scattered the nations across the face of the earth. He decided beforehand which should rise and fall, and when. He determined their boundaries. His purpose in all of this is that they should seek after God, and perhaps feel their way toward Him and find Him— though He is not far from any one of us. For in Him we live and move and are!" (Living)**

We must understand that once the Lord had finished creating every plant and animal and then said,

> **"Let us (Father, Son and Holy Spirit) make mankind after our image and our likeness",**

he was merely continuing with what he started when he told the plants and animals to multiply after themselves. Lastly, he would multiply and fill the earth.

The word "nations" in Acts 17:26 is the Greek word 'ethnos', which is our word 'ethnic'. By spreading people across the planet in different languages and cultures, he hoped that each ethnic group would seek and find him, and then express those elements of his character they'd discovered back to him in worship, and to other ethnic groups.

Thus, when you put the whole world together with each nation and ethnic group manifesting God's personality, like a prism in the light manifesting the whole spectrum of light, we have a much more complete picture of the Person of God.

Thus today, in broad generalizations, we can see the precision of the Germans, the engineering ability of the Dutch, the entrepreneurial abilities of the Americans, the worship of central Africa, and the strong families of Latin America as cultural and yet all are elements of God's personality demonstrated when these people come to the Lord. The numbers of ethnic groups in the earth range from 6,000 to over 20,000 depending on how they are categorized, and God's purpose was that each of these ethnic groups would seek God, feel after him and find him, thus reflecting a facet of God's own personality and character through and within their cultures.

Eventually, God's filling of the earth will be fulfilled when the voices in heaven can proclaim:

"The kingdoms of this world are become the kingdoms of our Lord, and of his Christ, and he shall reign for ever and ever." (Rev 11:15—KJV))

The reason we find life from the ocean floor to high in the air is that God has endowed each species with the ability to adapt to its' environment and occupy it. This ability stems from the Lord's command to multiply and fill the earth. He is attempting to do the same thing; fill whatever niche in mankind man will allow him.

The Lord is a Master at adapting to whatever structure man gives him.

Some church governments, like the Assembly's of God, are run like democracies. If 51% of the congregation votes the pastor out, he is out, yet God will seek to fill that structure to the fullest extent that structure will allow him. In one case the pastor wanted to raise money for a fellowship/youth building but there was one lady in the church opposed to it. She was able to stir up the congregation to not only defeat the proposal, but oust the pastor as well. Up until that time they had a growing youth program, but this lady opposed many of the more modern songs and was afraid more youth would continue to influence the worship music.

Though that pastor had to move on, God will still seek to fill whatever structure remains.

Many mega-churches are run like corporations or family businesses—God will fill that structure to whatever extent that structure allows him. One such church had a senior pastor that insisted within his family that his son follow in his footsteps, yet the son didn't want to. Still, the father pushed his son into the pulpit, headlining him next to his dad in larger meetings. One day the son rebelled and went off into the world, leaving no heir apparent. Yet God will still seek to fill whatever structure he is given, in spite of man's faults and foibles.

Some businesses are run by Christians and allow an expression of faith, or even Bible studies during lunch or break times—God will seek to fill whatever structure man gives him to the fullest extent that structure allows. The many Christian business organizations testify that there are many Godly business men and women who want to see God move in their workplace. The rise of what's called

"Marketplace" ministries is more evidence this is so. God will seek to fill whatever structure man gives Him to the fullest extent He can.

But the greatest structure, the one God originated himself in the beginning, was the individual and family in a home setting woven together in tight knit relationships. This structure allows him the greatest expression of His personality and freedom of movement. Thus, when Peter found himself with not one, but 3,120 temples of God, he did not try to take over the temple in Jerusalem, but rather continued in a way that allowed relationships to form and friendships to develop—the home and community. By this interconnecting community of disciples the multifaceted personality of God could be seen in the lives of thousands of individuals from all different cultures and life experiences.

The emphasis became relationships and the accountability that comes through those relationships, rather than structure. Note that immediately after Acts states there were about 3,000 new converts (though many were visitors):

> **"…they continued steadfastly in the apostles' doctrine and fellowship, and in the breaking of bread, and prayers. And they continued daily with one accord in the temple, and breaking bread from house to house, and did eat their meals with great joy and thankfulness." (Acts 2:41 & 46—KJV)**

Note that they were in the apostles' fellowship and teaching. The apostles were servants who went to the people, serving them by teaching and leading them. This is exactly opposite the temple set up where you had to go to the priests by appointment or other arrangement. Because we are each temples of God there is a respect for each other according to gifting rather than title, so the apostles made themselves available, traveling with others, to each other's homes. As Paul would note in Galatians 2:9:

> **"…and when James, Peter and John…<u>perceived the grace that was given to me</u>, they gave to me and Barnabus the right hands of fellowship; that we should go to the Gentiles and they to the Jews." (NKJV)**

In the home based New Testament church we are to perceive the grace given to each other, and it is upon that perception that we fellowship with each other. The apostles' fellowshipped with believers of all ethnic backgrounds and walks of life, perceiving the grace in them, and vice versa; thus seeing God Himself manifest through their testimonies and lives.

Transition time provided

It should be noted that Acts 2:46 mentions that the new believers met daily at the temple. We understand that this was a time of transition. The temple grounds had at its' center the sacrifice of animals and accompanying furniture and holy place. Around the temple were different courts and porches where the people gathered to hear various speakers and teachings. There were little covered pulpits in niches around the area in which groups of 20–50 could stand and hear speakers, which is what Jesus utilized in his day when the Bible tells us he taught in the temple. It was in this context that the new believers went to learn of their faith and the teachings of Jesus, with the apostles just continuing what they'd seen when they were with the Lord, and the text says they went from house to house as well.

This happy arrangement went on for about a year, or maybe two, and proved to be a great time of laying a foundation of knowledge in the hearts of the young church. Acts 8:1 indicates however these happy days didn't last long, for very shortly Steven was martyred:

> **"And Saul was consenting to his death. And at that time there was a great persecution against the church which was at Jerusalem; and <u>they were all</u> <u>scattered abroad throughout the regions of Judea and Samaria, except the</u> <u>apostles."</u> (KJV)**

Everyone, every convert from Pentecost and those added over the next year left Jerusalem because of the persecution that arose through Saul, the future apostle Paul. Once out of Jerusalem there were no temple grounds to gather together to hear Peter or James tell of their days with Jesus…everyone left town and were on their own, having to truly become 'a kingdom of priests' on their own in their own homes and communities.

God had given them a transition time of about a year or maybe two between Pentecost and Saul's persecution, allowing them time to digest the astounding revelation that they were now temples individually and didn't have to rely on God's presence in a building. If they had stayed in the temple mindset they would not have so readily moved out of town when the persecution arose.

I see this kind of transition time in the lives of many who are thinking about house church today, just as I was in the midst of transition as I thought on these things. Even while I was working and ministering within the traditional structure these observations and heart cry for more grew and developed deep within me.

I was earning my living in the traditional church, yet down in my heart I was in transition, shifting my focus away from the structure of how to do church and more onto God's people. At times I felt like a player on stage fulfilling a role, but in my heart and mind I felt like the stage crew behind the scenes scrambling around to bring about an orderly presentation. With so much churning around in me I needed a transition time to sort it all out. This was a positive transition; I wasn't backing away from something, I was running towards something much more wonderful. I wasn't retreating; I was marching forward, at first only in my mind and heart, but then physically, finding God outside the four walls of the church. I was seeing Him move in people from all walks of life in many different structures, and it was exciting and freeing for me.

It may take a year, maybe more, maybe less. There is a time where we must ponder the changes, the ramifications of those changes, and how we will walk them out. Some, like the early church, are forced out 'of town' so to speak, de-churched by a hierarchy that doesn't understand, but most come of it on their own, over time.

Chapter 2

Church in the House

Church in the House

As I studied I began to understand anew the reality of having Christ living in me, and what an amazing change in thinking it must have meant for the apostles. They had worshipped in the temple all their lives. They studied Moses and the Old Testament, and now the thought that the God who spoke to Moses on Mt. Sinai, the one who stood in the door to talk to Moses face to face, the one who traveled around as a pillar over the tabernacle, now lived in them!

Yet I could relate to them because even though mentally I understood that Christ lives in me, I was raised in a temple with a temple mentality. How often had I heard the preacher ask the congregation if it was good to be in God's house! Even though I mentally assented that God doesn't live in a building, somehow I still thought he did.

I realized the thing that drove the evangelistic efforts of New Testament leaders was the amazing revelation that God had moved out of the temple in Jerusalem and into individuals, accomplished through the work of Jesus' final blood sacrifice on the cross. His blood and vicarious sacrifice removed sin as an obstacle between God and man, tearing the veil, revealing that any who would, could not only enter into the holy place, but indeed become a holy place themselves!

I began to understand their perspective that truly, "…where two or three are gathered, there am I in the midst of them". Up until this point I knew that mentally, and I accepted that two friends could meet in someone's home and have a time of worship and Bible study—but that wasn't church. Or like my wife and I, when we were teenagers meeting with a group on Saturday nights for a time of worship and study at someone's house—but that wasn't church. Or was it?

My definition of church was changing, no longer connecting the gathering of disciples to a building as being church; I started looking at any meeting of purpose in which believers conducted the business of the kingdom as being church.

Houses in Acts

Once Saul becomes the apostle Paul in Acts 9, we next see that some returned to Jerusalem, for in Acts 12:12 a group of them are praying for Peter, who had just been released from prison by an angel:

> **"And when he had considered the thing, he came to the house of Mary the mother of John, whose surname was Mark; where many were gathered together praying." (KJV)**

I no longer saw this verse as just a part of scripture, I understood the logic and reasoning behind why they met in Mary's home for prayer—they were having, or rather being, church! No one was asking them who their covering was or what church they were associated with, they were just meeting freely for prayer for someone they loved!

The first house church in Philippi

In Acts 16 Paul has made his way into Greece, to the city of Philippi. The Jews of that city didn't have a synagogue, but they gathered at the river on the Jewish Sabbath, and Luke relates;

> **"…we sat down, and spoke to the women who had come there. And a certain woman named Lydia, a seller of purple, of the city of Thyatira who worshipped God, heard us: whose heart the Lord opened…She was baptized along with all her household and asked us to be her guests. "If you agree that I am faithful to the Lord," she said, "come and stay at my home." (Living)**

This became the founding of the church at Philippi, with Lydia's home as the main house where church was held. Even after Paul and Silas' experience of being beaten and thrown in jail, only to see their shackles drop off them by an earthquake as they sang praises to God at midnight, they went back to Lydia's house upon release (16:40):

"Paul and Silas returned to the home of Lydia where they met with the believers and preached to them once more before leaving town." (Living)

From there, Acts 17:1 records Paul going immediately to Thessalonica. At some point later he wrote back to Lydia and the church in her house and other believers (the jailer and his household for instance), and that is what we call the letter to the Philippians. It is Paul's warmest and most personal of letters, and he even says in 4:16 how they supported him in the ministry:

"As you well know, when I first brought the Gospel to you and then went on my way, leaving Macedonia, only you Philippians became my partners in giving and receiving. No other church did this. Even when I was over in Thessalonica you sent help twice." (Living)

The first house church in Thessalonica

In Thessalonica Paul initially gained converts by teaching Jesus in the synagogue in the city. Acts 17:2 says he spent three Saturdays convincing them Jesus was the Messiah, but while some believed, others did not. Verse 4 says

"...and of the devout Greeks a great multitude, and of the chief women, not a few." (KJV)

But trouble was being stirred up by the unbelieving Jews, for in verse 5 it states:

"...and set all the city on an uproar, and <u>assaulted the house of Jason, and</u> <u>sought to bring them out</u> to the people. And when they found them not, they drew Jason and certain brethren to the rulers of the city...and when they had taken security of Jason, and of the other, they let them go. And the brethren immediately sent away Paul and Silas by night..." (KJV)

Author C. Peter Wagner, in his commentary on the book of Acts says this:

"This church, <u>like all the others Paul planted, began as one house church</u>, in all probability meeting in the house of a man named

Jason (Acts 17:5). Jason is a Greek name, so he was more than likely one of the God-fearers who heard Paul preach for three Sabbaths in the synagogue. Probably not long after Paul left, the number of house churches in Thessalonica began to multiply, spreading out from their base in Jason's house. The Thessalonian believers were aggressively evangelistic because Paul writes to them a few months later, saying, 'For from you the word of the Lord has sounded forth, not only in Macedonia and Achaia, but also in every place.' (I Thess. 1:8)" (pg 419)

Paul penned I and II Thessalonians shortly after he had to leave Jason and the believers, and sent Timothy back to Thessalonica to see how they were doing. (I Thess 3:2)

The house churches at Corinth

We next see houses mentioned as the place for church in Acts 18 and the founding of the church at Corinth. Paul became business partners with a couple named Aquila and Priscilla (Prisca), who were tentmakers by trade like Paul, and became close ministry companions. (18:1–3)

This couple is mentioned six times in the New Testament, and in most versions Priscilla is mentioned first in four of those six times, indicating she was the main speaker. Just as in today's culture, many know of Joyce and Dave Meyer or Marilyn and Wally Hickey, these women teachers are better known than their husbands. They aren't usurping authority, for their husbands recognize their call and encourage them to flow in their gifts, even as they do theirs (Dave being an administrator and Wally being the pastor).

As Paul's custom was, offering salvation first to the Jews, he entered into the synagogue until their opposition caused him to say:

"Your blood is upon your own heads; I am clean: from henceforth I will go to the Gentiles. And he left there and <u>entered into a certain man's house</u>, <u>named Justus</u>, whose house joined hard to the synagogue. And Crispus the chief ruler of the synagogue, <u>believed on the Lord with his entire house</u>. " (18:6–8—NKJV))

Some texts list Justus as Titius Justus, and was probably also named Gaius, Paul's host in Romans 16:23. It is not unusual for Romans to have three names, and

Paul mentioned in I Corinthians 3:14, that in Corinth he baptized only Crispus, Gaius, and the household of Stephanas.

Like the church at Thessalonica, it appears Justus/Gaius and Crispus were leaders; one Roman believer and one Jewish believer, and the church grew to other houses as believers were added.

House churches in Rome

From Corinth Paul went to Ephesus, but it is interesting to note that Paul would again visit Corinth during his 3rd journey, maybe some six years later, mentioned in Acts 20:1–4. It is during this time that he wrote his letter to the Romans from Corinth.

In Romans 16:1 he mentions a woman deaconess named Phoebe from nearby Cenchrea, just down the road from Corinth, who probably carried Paul's letter to the Romans. By this time Aquila and Priscilla have returned to Rome, and Paul says in 16:5 to,

"…greet the church that is in their house." (KJV)

In Romans 16:21 he also relays greetings from Jason, who we saw in Acts 17:5 hosting the church at Thessalonica in his home, now perhaps a traveling companion with Paul.

Romans 16:22–23 are worth noting as well.

"I Tertius, who wrote this epistle, salute you in the Lord. Gaius (Justus) my host, and of the whole church salutes you. Erastus the treasurer of the city salutes you, and Quartus, a brother." (NKJV)

Here we see that Paul dictated his letter to the Romans as was his custom, employing a man named Tertius as his secretary. He mentions the Treasurer of the city of Corinth, and Quartus, a brother. In the Roman Empire, when they would take a slave, they took away that person's name. Then they branded them with a number, either on their forehead or wrist. The name 'Tertius' is the Roman number 'three', and the name Quartus is the Roman number 'four'. Archeological digs have discovered engravings in the ancient city of Corinth bearing the name of Erastus as Treasurer.

Thus we see the beauty of perceiving the grace of God in individuals, for Paul had no trouble mixing and mingling with the Treasurer of the city and 2 slaves, nor any problem with a woman being a leader in the church in Cenchrea or the church in Philippi. Aside from these examples, he mentions two relatives (husband and wife) in Romans 16:7, Andronicus and Junia, who were in Christ before him and whom he calls apostles. He also mentions Mary (v6), Tryphaena and Tryphosa and Persis (v12) and Julia (v15).

Paul truly lived by the principle mentioned in Galatians 2:9 that the Christian life, the key to walking in love, is to perceive the grace of God in each other recognizing God's work in a believer's life rather than focusing on office or gender or other qualifying factor.

House Churches in Ephesus

From Paul's first visit to Corinth he went to Ephesus. He found about 12 men who were disciples of John the Baptist, not having heard of Jesus, but Paul quickly remedied that situation. Additionally, he went to the synagogue and taught about Jesus over the span of three months, which would have been 12 Saturdays. (Acts 19:1–8)

In a unique move, but one that shows that individuals are temples and God is willing to fill whatever structure man gives him to flow through, Paul moved into a school, owned and run by a man named Tyrannus.

Ephesus in Paul's time had an estimated population of 250,000 people, which meant it was the fourth largest city in the empire after Rome, Alexandria, and Antioch of Syria. (Clinton Arnold, Ephesians: Power and Magic; Grand Rapids, MI: Baker Book House, 1992, p6)

To once again quote C. Peter Wagner's commentary on the book of Acts (p469):

"The Western text of the Greek New Testament tells us that Paul taught from the fifth to the tenth hour, or from 11am to 4pm every day."

This would be in keeping with the known custom in the Mediterranean region of a siesta from 11am–4pm, having worked from sun up until the heat of the day, then returning to finish work after 4pm in the cool of the afternoon until sundown, allowing students to spend their siesta time at Bible school. Over the next two years the Gospel spread through all the province of Asia, which was in Paul's time a state in the western part of Turkey.

There are no specific individuals or their homes mentioned in Ephesus like we have in Philippi, Thessalonica, Corinth or Rome, but in Acts 20:20, at a meeting of the leaders of Ephesus Paul says:

"And how I kept back nothing that was profitable to you, but have showed you and have taught you publicly (Bible school) and from <u>house to house</u>…" (KJV)

So we can see that when Paul was writing his epistle to the Ephesians, like the ones mentioned above, he was writing to people meeting in homes all over the city and province of Asia.

Paul's house in Rome

From Acts 20:20 until chapter 28 Luke follows the journeys of Paul as he makes his way to Rome, the largest part of those chapters showing Paul a prisoner of Rome, thus no church planting is mentioned. However, once in Rome Acts 28:16 and 28:30–31 tell of Paul's own home being a central location for learning of the Lord:

"And when we came to Rome…Paul was allowed to live by himself with the soldier that guarded him…And he lived there two whole years at his own expense, and welcomed all who came to him, preaching the kingdom of God, and teaching those things about the Lord Jesus Christ, quite openly and unhindered." (Revised Standard)

Other house churches mentioned in Paul's letters

As Paul closes his letter to the churches at Colossae he makes this request in Col 4:15:

"Give my greetings to the brethren at Laodicea, and to Nympha and the assembly (the church) <u>which meets in her house</u>." (AMP)

Paul wrote his shortest letter to a man named Philemon, who was a member of the church at Colossae. We know this because the subject of his letter to Philemon, Onesimus, is also mentioned in Colossians 4:9. Onesimus was a run away slave who met Paul, whether by design or accident we don't know, in Rome, and Paul was sending Onesimus back to Philemon with a letter hoping to smooth the way for him. In verses one and two of his letter to Philemon Paul says:

> **"Paul, a prisoner (for the sake) of Christ Jesus, the Messiah, and our brother Timothy, to Philemon our dearly loved sharer with us in our work, and to Apphia our sister and Archippus our fellow soldier (in the Christian warfare), <u>and to the church (assembly that meets) in your house…</u>"** (AMP)

Priscilla and Aquilla seemed to travel quite a bit, and it would seem wherever they settled they held church in their house, for yet again, writing from Ephesus in 59AD to the churches in Corinth Paul says of them:

> **"The churches of Asia greet you. Aquila and Priscilla greet you much in the Lord, with the church that is in their house."** (KJV) (I Cor 16:19)

Additional home based events that happened in Acts include Saul going into the houses to arrest Christians (8:3); Cornelius seeing an angel while at prayer in his house and Peter's visit to that house resulted in the Holy Spirit filling everyone present (10:44); Paul received a direct Word from God through the prophet Agabus while meeting at Philip's house (21:8–11); the household of Stephanas was among the first converts of that region of Greece (I Cor 16:15); and Paul cautions busy bodies going from house to house (I Tim 5:13). Clearly the church was based in the home and the home was the focal point of ministry.

A new understanding of the New Testament

Once we understand that Paul's letters, not to mention Peter, James, John, Jude as well as the Gospel writers, were all writing to people who met in homes throughout the Roman Empire, we must reset our minds to understand that context. Also, understanding that Paul worked with men and women alike, treating them equally, as demonstrated by his acceptance of Lydia hosting the church in Philippi, Nymphas in Colossae, Junia mentioned as an apostle and Phoebe as a deaconess, among others, it brings into balance difficult scriptures which, when placed in the context of a first century living room suddenly make sense.

As I examined the reality of house church around the world, both past and present, I realized the context of the New Testament—from the Gospel of Matthew to The Revelation—these letters were written to people sitting in living rooms as guests in someone's home. This meant social etiquette should be followed, and there was no place for confusion or impropriety.

God in the house was God's plan from the Garden through The Revelation, not just a principle for the founding of the church and throughout the Roman world. The letters of the New Testament which I have pored over and memorized and loved since I was a teenager, were all written to people who met in homes. The sudden realization of that fact unleashed a flood of emotions on the inside of me. Why wasn't I taught this in Bible school? Why wasn't this taught from the pulpits of the traditional church?

I further realized that in church and Bible school I had, for some 25 years filtered my understanding of the New Testament through the temple philosophy of Constantine instead of the house based teachings of Paul! I was horrified!

Suddenly I understood why no letters of the New Testament were written to leaders but were instead written to everyone…"the church at". Suddenly I understood why Paul told the Corinthians that **they** should have dealt with the man sleeping with his step mother in I Corinthians 5, and that **they** should settle the issue between two brothers suing each other in court amongst themselves. Not once did Paul or other writers of the New Testament tell the leaders to handle it as I would have in my filtering through the temple mentality. Paul advocated personal responsibility among the people through mutual submission to each other and the Lord guided by love and social etiquette and customs.

When I realized all this and that Romans, I & II Corinthians, Ephesians, Philippians, Colossians, I & II Thessalonians, and Philemon were written to people who were named specifically as hosting church in their homes (or school), I wondered, how did we stray so far over the course of centuries when it's so clearly laid out for us?

Chapter 3

The Pyramid

The Pyramid System

Once I understood that church was originally in the home and that all over the world house churches were exploding, as well as understanding the basic structure, I began to examine the structure of the traditional church. I found it to be a pyramid. The more I traveled in ministry the more I found common traits within these pyramids. But let me explain.

The 'pyramid' that I refer to is the traditional church structure that came into being when Constantine called the people from their homes and into the formerly pagan temples. This format closely resembles the 'Jethro principle' of Exodus 18: 13–27. Israel had just passed through the Sea as a new nation and had no internal structure, no federal government.

As a result, Moses had been judging disputes from sun up to sun down and Jethro, Moses' father in law, advised him to set up 'rulers of thousands, rulers of hundreds, rulers of fifties, and rulers of tens' (18:24). This placed Moses at the top of a pyramid, overseeing men with varying degrees of authority, all answering to the 'ruler' above them. This became the Federal government of Israel, while later on the Lord would establish the priesthood and tabernacle for religious worship, but Jethro's instructions became the basic governmental structure of the new nation.

"…Listen now to me…You shall represent the people before God, bringing their cases and causes to Him. Moreover you shall choose able men from all the people—God-fearing men…and make them rulers of

thousands, rulers of hundreds, rulers of fifties, and rulers of tens. And let them judge the people at all times; every great matter they shall bring to you, but every small matter they shall judge…" (Ex 18:19–22 AMP)

Every traditionally structured church—from the denominational church to the charismatic to the evangelical—are all patterned after the Jethro principle, with one person at the top overseeing 'rulers' of varying degrees of authority. This structure is a line down, ruling from above dictation of the vision and direction for an organization.

By virtue of the pastor being at the top of the pyramid, it means he is often inaccessible to the 'common' people, just as Moses shut himself off from the day to day struggles of everyday man, delegating their care to the 'rulers'. Jethro told Moses:

"You shall represent the people before God, bringing their cases and causes to Him, Teaching them the decrees and laws, showing them the way they must walk and the work they must do." (Ex 18:19–20 AMP)

This is why for centuries Christians have depended on their pastor to tell them what God is saying. It makes for a very weak, lazy, and ignorant body of Christ, but that has been the structure of church for some 1700 years.

However, Jethro's pyramid was valid in Moses' day because it was the formation of a civil government. Jethro recognized that Israel needed a government and suggested the pyramid. It was never intended to be a model for the church, and certainly wasn't followed by Paul or the other writers of the New Testament.

Jethro's Pyramid, the structure of all traditional churches since about 313AD

The characteristics listed in the following pages vary only by degree and frequency determined by the size of the church or ministry. I've seen these traits in churches of 25 people and mega churches, it's the structure that is inherently flawed and at odds with what God intended for the church to be, therefore these elements are common no matter the size.

Let me also acknowledge that God moves in traditionally structured churches, for he will seek to fill whatever structure man gives him to the fullest extent he can, yet it cannot be denied that God is moving in a new way today. It's just that the 'new way' of house church is really the original way of doing church as an

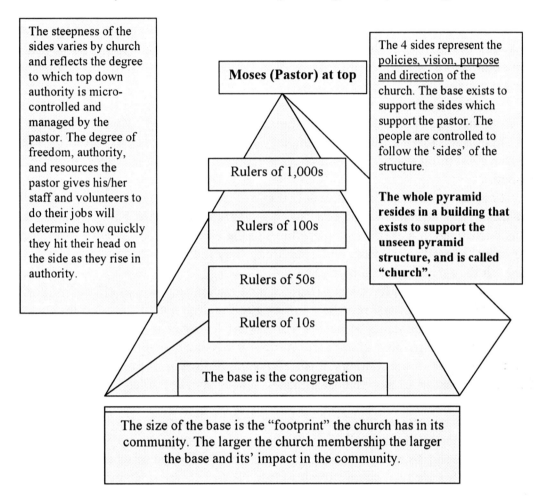

The steepness of the sides varies by church and reflects the degree to which top down authority is micro-controlled and managed by the pastor. The degree of freedom, authority, and resources the pastor gives his/her staff and volunteers to do their jobs will determine how quickly they hit their head on the side as they rise in authority.

The 4 sides represent the policies, vision, purpose and direction of the church. The base exists to support the sides which support the pastor. The people are controlled to follow the 'sides' of the structure.

The whole pyramid resides in a building that exists to support the unseen pyramid structure, and is called "church".

Moses (Pastor) at top

Rulers of 1,000s

Rulers of 100s

Rulers of 50s

Rulers of 10s

The base is the congregation

The size of the base is the "footprint" the church has in its community. The larger the church membership the larger the base and its' impact in the community.

extension of the family unit and as practiced by the founding apostles and New Testament. It's merely a return to our spiritual roots.

Characteristics and issues inherent within the Jethro Pyramid

If you were inside the pyramid you could ascend straight up in rank and authority, but would eventually run into a side wall running at an angle to the very top. The sides represent the policies, vision, purpose and direction of the church and all four lean together to form the point at the top, which supports the pastor. The base represents the members in the pews. The base also represents the size and scope of the ministry, as well as the degree to which the person at the top of the pyramid controls it all through the communication of the 4 sides (policy, vision, purpose and direction). The base is occupied by the average person in the pew.

As a person rises in authority from the base, becoming 'ruler' over more, they will eventually hit their head on the angled side of the pyramid. Somewhere, somehow, a policy, vision, purpose or direction of the church will rub against the person moving up.

If the base is very wide, often the sides will be shallow, with anyone moving up from the base immediately hitting their heads on a side wall. That church may be spread thin and there is much micromanagement or heavy rules and regulations that govern everything done in the church. A person rising up will feel very tightly controlled.

A haggard and worn out couple came to me in desperation. They were helping their pastor start a church and they only had about 15 people, but this couple was exhausted. They did absolutely everything in the church while the pastor did nothing other than give direction, and everything they did was scrutinized to the point they felt they could do nothing right.

Some churches have steep sides, which may mean there is greater authority and latitude given to staff members before running into a side wall, yet the overall scope of the ministry maybe have a very small footprint in the community. This could be something like a church, TV ministry, mission agency or other ministry in which the focus of the ministry is all about the big name at the top. Again, these traits are common to any size of ministry that is focused solely on the pastor or leader at the top.

The steepness to the sides of the pyramid is determined by the strong will and drive of the head person. Whether the pyramid is very steep or shallow, the same principles apply: To move up in the pyramid eventually one must sacrifice part of himself and his identity, submitting it to 'the vision' or 'the man' or 'the call' at the top. In the end, the pyramid is all about "Moses" and his or her vision.

Changing Direction

No matter the steepness of the sides, if you want to make your way towards the top, you must change direction once you hit a side wall; you must change from moving only vertically to making a move sideways. Herein lies the compromise; moving sideways means you give up part of yourself, your giftings, and your higher purpose in Christ to submit them to the policies, vision, purpose, or direction of the church or ministry.

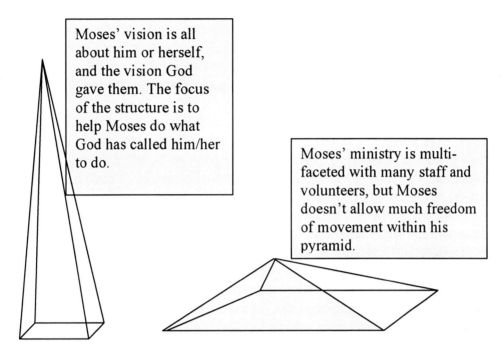

Moses' vision is all about him or herself, and the vision God gave them. The focus of the structure is to help Moses do what God has called him/her to do.

Moses' ministry is multi-faceted with many staff and volunteers, but Moses doesn't allow much freedom of movement within his pyramid.

I am not saying to do so is to have ulterior motives or in any way suggesting that everyone who moves up in a pyramid is doing so to enlarge their territory, but I am saying that the nature of the pyramid is political. To move up in the pyramid means you might have more freedom to do what is on your heart to do within the system as it lines up with the pastor's vision, which makes the risk worth taking.

In the same way Moses' rulers over 10 would have liked to be over 50 and then maybe to 100 or even 1000, our churches are filled with volunteers and staff members hoping to move up, which means not only will they have more authority to do what is on their heart, but they will be in charge of someone who is over 10 or 50 or 100.

I do believe many who are in the pyramid church are happy and in God's will, as I was for many years. It was the only system I knew and I was happy to work within it, but I was always wondering if some of my own dreams would be able to come to pass within the various pyramids I served.

God's will thwarted, detour for us

Years ago the Lord led my wife and I to attend a church of about 250 people and soon I was asked to be the Associate Pastor. The church owned 14 acres and had a nice facility with plenty of room to expand. Both the pastor and I had the vision of starting a Bible school and missionary training center and we were eager to begin. The pastor also owned two businesses he was going to sell and then resign from pastoring the church to concentrate on the school and missionary training, living off the profits from the sale of his businesses. At that point I would become the Senior Pastor.

My wife and I knew it was the Lord's will that we be at that church, and I was more than willing to be the Associate Pastor until the day I was elevated to the position of Senior Pastor. My heart was on the soon-to-be Bible school and the discipling process of adult students as well as giving spiritual guidance to members of the congregation.

I hurt for the people I couldn't get to, and the pastor being wrapped up in his businesses really didn't have a pastoral heart for the people nor the time to deal with them. My wife and I longed for the day I would be the Senior Pastor so we could reach so many more people who needed our help.

But one day the Pastor visited my wife and I and said that he decided not to sell his businesses because once all the bills were paid he would only have $750,000 left over, "…and you can't do anything for God with only $750,000." He was going to stay on as Senior Pastor and I was in a dead end position. We knew he was missing the Lord and by the Spirit knew the church would go under and he would lose his businesses as well if he didn't obey God's plan, but there was nothing we could do. Soon after we were told that we were the third couple he had made these promises to.

We began praying for a new church for us that needed a true pastor while silently mourning for the people of that church and the vision for the Bible school and training center that would never happen. Heartbroken, we went to the Lord on what we were to do with our lives and he spoke to my wife: "I tried to work through men's hearts but they would not allow me, so I have to work around them. However, because it was through no fault of your own, you will remain in my perfect will, but it will mean a detour." A few months later a church opened up about 3 hours away and the Lord blessed us in our time there, but I still wonder what could have been at the other church.

Perhaps the reader has been in such a place where events and people conspired to stop the direction of God for a church or ministry and you were caught in the middle as we were. Perhaps you had to make a detour as well.

This is the Jethro system. To move up means you move sideways first, putting your own dreams on hold in order to serve the person at the top, or the vision of the person at the top, and if they miss it or step out of the love and will of God, those 'rulers' within the pyramid will suffer.

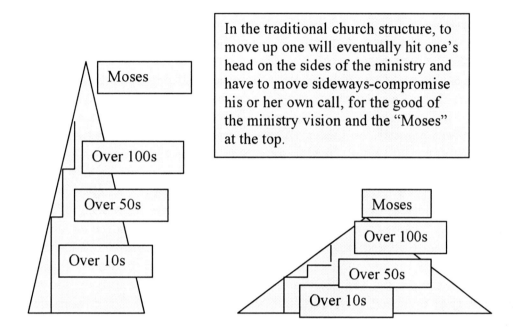

In the traditional church structure, to move up one will eventually hit one's head on the sides of the ministry and have to move sideways-compromise his or her own call, for the good of the ministry vision and the "Moses" at the top.

The reward for this sideways move is that you get to stay within the pyramid, making a name and territory for yourself. For many within this system, often everything else from this point on is done either to maintain position, or continue to move up by manipulating the system and person at the top to get your way.

Remember that the Jethro principle establishes these territories. My territory over fifty people is greater than your territory over ten, but I must submit myself to the one who is over the hundreds. Therefore I will protect my realm within the pyramid lest I be demoted or find myself outside the pyramid. Even in small churches I've seen people in charge of the nursery or children's church get so caught up in their own importance they make helping in that church miserable for everyone under their authority. The principles are the same because of the structure common to all traditional churches.

Un-funded Mandates

Because the person at the top of the pyramid wants to stay at the top and keep the organization moving, he must control each person within the pyramid. Therefore people below are not truly empowered to flow within their own gifts, though they still yearn for recognition and value, which sets up many conflicts within a church employee or volunteer.

By giving a person a title but little authority and few resources to do the job, (whether purposeful or just a lack of money) nevertheless it becomes possible for the leadership at the top to demand results and hold them accountable without having to make the resources available to the volunteer or employee. A person with a title often has no real financial authority over his or her department. Several Financial Officers in various churches and ministries have told me the same story; a ministry really has only about 7%–11% leeway in their finances. The other 89%–93% is usually tied up in staff, buildings, programs and so forth. Thus most churches and other ministries can't really afford to give their staff and volunteers a lot of financial freedom within their department because the fixed costs are so high. One time I became pastor of a church that had a set policy that the pastor received 40% of all tithes and offerings as his salary. All other expenses were to have been taken out of the remaining 60%, leaving very little for materials for the children or nursery, or other programs. I immediately did away with that policy, instead choosing a set salary for myself, but the mindset of the original was to spur the pastor to get more money from the people, and the more money from them the more for the pastor! Fixed costs of overhead, programs, and salaries is why even large ministries are extremely sensitive to the giving from the congregation or ministry partners, even a drop of 7% puts the church on the verge of not being able to pay its' bills, thus the continual push in many churches for tithing and giving that becomes so wearing on the soul.

One lady was involved in a Saturday morning neighborhood outreach at her church. The program consisted of a panel truck with the side hinged so that when it opened the interior of the truck was a puppet stage. The people involved would pull into a neighborhood playing music similar to an ice cream truck, stop on the curb and lower the side of the truck and start a puppet show, with the conclusion offering a prayer of salvation and printed children's material and candy.

The program was much touted from the pulpit, but there was little support beyond that. The time and hoops to jump through whenever they needed money for materials was so great they ended up buying it themselves. It set up a huge conflict within these dedicated volunteers and staff members who couldn't understand why they couldn't get the money to support such a worthy program that could document many children praying the prayer of salvation.

Often a pyramid structured church must rotate what department or outreach is in the limelight and raise funds for it, or keep a building program before the people in order to keep the money flowing in, because just the day to day 'regular' giving doesn't always pay the bills.

This can prove to be emotionally and spiritually challenging for other programs or departments within a church as they watch other programs receive special offerings while they sit back with nothing extra. Because of the lines of authority of the rulers, this arbitrary focus of attention on other departments according to the needs of the pastor at the top can make those within the structure jealous and have attitudes towards those departments and workers that seem to be the favored ones.

One church of about 125 people soothed feelings along these lines by having a ministry and volunteer Sunday in which each department took turns in lieu of a Sermon that week sharing what they were doing and encouraged people to get involved. One lady still complained to me afterwards; "I don't know if anything will come of it. We're up there and get people all excited about what we're doing and then another department comes up after us and gets them stirred up about what they're doing!"

The need for attention

The rulers in Moses' pyramid had very limited amount of authority—just what pertained to their tens or fifties or hundreds or thousands—but Moses oversaw them, and by extension, the millions. But Jethro's instructions to Moses were to let the underlings deal with the day to day decisions, and let the harder ones be passed up the line until only the hardest decisions actually came to Moses' desk. Moses only dealt with the few rulers at the top, and was out of touch with the real day to day operations of the nation.

Thus we have churches all over the world with volunteers and staff members who have said or think: "Pastor doesn't even know what really goes on in his church." Or perhaps they've thought, "If Pastor really knew what went on he would be angry." I've heard those exact comments from people volunteering in a church of 45 as well as staff members in mega-churches. Moses can't know what's going on because of the basic structure of the pyramid. People instinctively know this, yet they wonder if pastor really does know (what goes on) but turns a deaf ear and blind eye. It is the structure that is flawed; the people usually have good and right hearts, but know of no other system for doing church.

The person low on the line of authority, the person over 10 or 50, has little contact with 'Moses' and therefore can't communicate their needs or the great job they are doing for God. They are urged to 'believe God' for basic supplies and resources in order to fulfill the demands of the mandate coming down from above, but have very limited access to anyone with enough authority to help them and their efforts.

Can I get an appointment with you pastor?

Even trying to get an appointment with the pastor is like running the gauntlet in most churches over about 300 people. The upper level staff continually tries to pawn a person off to a lower ruler, but only the most determined will be rewarded with that cherished prize, an appointment with the pastor alone in his office, 1 on 1.

It's sad that I've seen so many staff members and volunteers over the years proclaim how they know the pastor and his wife very well, that they've even been in their house or spoken to them directly about the problems in their department. Like a badge of honor worn so all may see, they revel in their 15 minutes of fame, and reveal yet again the failures of the current church system of the pyramid.

And when you leave

When a person leaves a church or ministry they often discover they don't have a clue what to do with their lives as it pertains to serving God. One young lady worked very hard in a church outreach to children in a low income neighborhood. She loved the children and they needed help, so it was a good fit. But when the ministry changed pastors that program was dropped, and she found herself in a spiritual desert without direction or purpose.

She had given up part of herself for those children and that program, and she did so before she really knew herself and her own call. Like the character Maggie in the movie "Runaway Bride" who liked her eggs cooked the way each of her several boyfriends like them but had to discover on her own how she liked her eggs, so too this young lady had to discover her own call and purpose aside from any church program.

If people would be able to flow in their call and vision within the pyramid instead of having to lay it down for a season to serve Moses' vision, they could leave that church or ministry and pick right up with their own call. As it is, often that person feels lost and without direction, having never known or perhaps forgotten God's call and purpose for their life that he told them years before.

Conflict in the heart

Within the lower level rulers a conflict arises between those who aren't on their way to the top and those who want to move up to the next level. They see the politics and hate it, yet they derive their living or sense of fulfillment from the organization. They stay because they are working for God, not man, and they must 'hunker down' for the duration, keeping their eyes peeled for the day God would open up their promotion or something else.

At the same time, the person in the pew not involved in any program or the ministry partner if the ministry is not a church, will not know all the elements that go on within the upper levels of the pyramid. These people are blissfully in the dark. The only time one of these people might be able to see the politics involved is if they become a volunteer or employee of the church or ministry. Then they go through a difficult time of discovering their favorite minister and their organization is not heaven on earth, but rather made of clay, like themselves.

Years ago I worked for a large ministry with a huge retreat and conference center under development. We would have families drive up in pick up trucks with all their belongings in the back and proclaim, "God told us to come so where do you want us to live?" We would have to tell them that the Lord didn't tell us they were coming, and our suggestion would be to find a place to live and jobs, or apply for a job within the ministry, and see what doors the Lord might open.

More often than not these people would never be seen again, but sometimes their call to be there was genuine and they would become a co-worker. I spent many hours helping these wonderfully idealistic people with hearts of gold work through the disappointment that the business of the ministry was just that, a business. Thinking they would be in regular touch with the leaders, they discovered they were hired to do a job, and would be better off if they would work as unto the Lord and keep a good attitude.

I wonder how many rulers over Moses' 10 or 50 or 100 thought they might have regular contact with Moses? What did they go through when they discovered their job was basically the complaint department and there was little room for advancement?

The Culture of Fear

The nature of the pyramid produces a mindset of 'either you're for us or against us' in the minds of those who love that particular church or ministry. Often it manifests as a matter of loyalty seen in church attendance, paying your tithes, and saying 'yes' to whatever the pastor says.

I know of churches that have the congregation shout "We're a 100% tithing church" during offering and some even have volunteers submit their tax returns so they can be sure they are tithing.

Other pastors tell their congregations that they expect their members to only attend their church and forbid them from attending another church, even if there is a guest speaker at some evening service.

For the leaders performance and appearance means everything. For volunteers or staff members it means being afraid to do something wrong. This in turn sets up an atmosphere of fear and intimidation when the head man is near. A man on the pastoral staff at a church said he just had to keep his nose to his job and he dared not say anything to his boss who was overseer of all the pastoral staff, lest he be labeled disloyal or having an attitude. He was frustrated that no one was willing to be able to bring up real issues that might produce positive change, but had seen what happened to those who did.

At a staff retreat of his church, the senior pastor told everyone that he wanted everyone to be truthful in work and that they should feel free to bring up issues and suggestions for change. A week later one staff member took the pastor at his word and wrote up several suggestions to his boss. About three days later the man was fired, accused of being disloyal and having an attitude, no longer in agreement with the vision of the ministry.

Everyone is afraid that something isn't 'just right' because they know they will be called on the carpet for it. I know a person who was on the pastoral staff of one such organization who was pulled aside on two separate occasions within 6 months of each other by church members wanting to know why there was such fear in the staff members when the pastor came near. The stronger the pyramid structures the more fear and heavy handedness from the top, and again, the size of the structure doesn't matter, the symptoms are the same.

Coupled with the hierarchy and culture of fear is the reality that the lower ones in authority have many bosses. A ruler of 10 will do what his boss, the ruler over 50 told him to do, but then a ruler over 100 or 1,000 will come along and countermand the previous order with the hapless staff member getting chewed out by his original boss for not doing what he was told.

This often happens with volunteers and in facilities/janitorial and maintenance staff. While setting up an auditorium for a Wednesday night service, the set up crew was told to move a section of hundreds of chairs back more by someone above their boss in rank, only to be told later by someone higher than him that pastor wanted a more close in and intimate set up so move the chairs in. Then the crew got chewed out by their original boss who had a real fit before they could explain why they had disobeyed him. Such is the pyramid.

It also means employees and volunteers can't go down front at an altar call for fear that they may be seen as needy, or weak. Appearance is everything and to have an employee receive prayer would indicate something is wrong with them, the church or the system.

Anytime an employee or volunteer seeks to address real issues they may be branded as 'not being on board' or having an attitude. The person becomes frustrated because no one in a position of authority will talk straight about the needs of the organization or department, they only spiritualize true issues, leaving the person with no where to turn.

The Leader has a Non-stick Coating

This sets up the leader to be 'Teflon', meaning nothing sticks to him or her. They have their associate(s) who plays the heavy and puts the proper spin on the latest problem. The spin ignores the true issues and everyone in the pyramid except the congregation can see through it, but everyone knows the head man cannot be guilty of sin or politics, so nothing sticks to him. When decisions are made that may be controversial it's done in a group setting so 'they' can be said to have made the decision, not the main man. But when something positive happens it came directly from God to the leader.

This sets up the structure that makes all meetings of leadership nothing more than a rubber stamp on what the leader wants. There is no true discussion of the issues, only praise reports and minor decisions to be made as a group. The real issues are made with the pastor and 1 or 2 others, the top administrators being kept in the dark on purpose by the leader.

Anyone in a meeting that seeks to speak his or her own opinion is questioned later and confronted by leadership. They want to know why they didn't say the same thing as everyone else. Again, they have given up part of their own identity to stay within the pyramid.

Annual Changing of the Guard

Another of the symptoms is high turnover. When you see a ministry with high turnover, you have a pyramid with a broad base and low side walls, indicating extreme control issues. An amazing contrast can be seen when one looks at the Billy Graham organization with many, many employees who have been with the ministry multiple decades versus many churches that have an annual ritual of 'out with the old and in with the new'.

One elder in a large church expressed concern about the turn over in staff and church membership. He said the whole congregation turned over every 1 1/2 years or 2, meaning that except for the core group, the whole congregation was all new that often.

His quest became trying to find a solution to 'shutting the back door' of the church, both in staff and membership. He never found a solution because that's the nature of the pyramid.

Defectors

As a person is faced with the choice of giving up his or her own identity to move up within an organization a funny thing happens: Some people choose to move outside the pyramid and/or find other employment or start attending another church, thinking that pyramid will be different.

A church member who isn't part of the pyramid structure may just want to move on to a new church, but often they make a terrifying discovery: Some within the pyramid look down upon those who move out, and they ostracize those who leave, feeling like they can't socialize with 'the defector'. One lady approached me because she worked with a woman who had left her church and the pastor, from the pulpit, had told people not to associate with her because she had left the church. The woman who approached me was afraid and confused because she worked with the woman that left and didn't know how to act. I told her to ignore her pastor, when she's at work they're paying her to work with this woman.

I've spoken to dozens of people who have the same story: They had very close and good relationships with people at their former church and thought those friendships were forever, but they discovered as soon as they moved to another church the friendships ended.

They were horrified to discover that they had thought more of the people they loved at that church than those people felt about them. The hurt and anguish stays with people for years. Made to feel like they did something wrong, or worse, not knowing what they did wrong, they reluctantly admit they didn't know their friendships were based on church membership or employment there and nothing else. Again, this is just the nature of the pyramid at work; the reason you are in the pyramid is to fulfill the vision of the Moses at the top, and relationships begin and end within that system.

How sad that pastors, in an effort to maintain control, resort to demonizing those who leave their church. Sometimes it's open, other times pastors make remarks without naming names, but in such a way everyone knows who he or she is talking about. This is evil. Again, it's a symptom of the Jethro pyramid structure and the need to maintain control over people.

The bases touch, which means the people in the pews flow back and forth, and for year's people have prayed for their city that the pastors will get together so they can win their town for Christ. Yet as illustrated by the pyramids above, the tops can never meet just by the nature of the structure. Thus other than a few friendships between pastors and token pulpit exchanges or community services between churches and pastors, each pyramid still does it's own thing independent of the other churches in town.

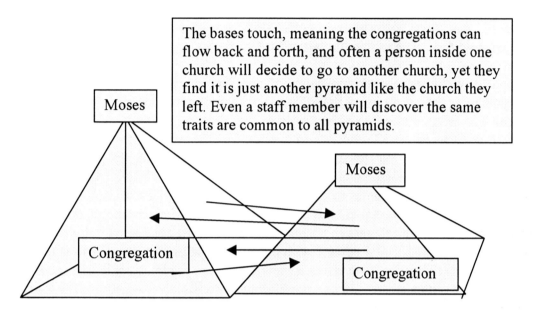

The bases touch, meaning the congregations can flow back and forth, and often a person inside one church will decide to go to another church, yet they find it is just another pyramid like the church they left. Even a staff member will discover the same traits are common to all pyramids.

A pyramid structure is populated largely by maintainers rather than creative people.

Many people with drive, creativity, an entrepreneurial spirit, an 'apostolic' call or perhaps even for reasons of integrity move out to continue in their walk with God. They cannot abide within the pyramid any longer because they are no longer willing to give up that part of themselves that is most basic to their life, their call and higher purpose in life.

That's not to say everyone who leaves a church or ministry is dissatisfied, indeed many move on because their hearts have become larger than the vision of the pyramid of which they've been a part. They recognize the dissatisfaction as God working within them to enlarge their vision, and are able to keep a positive attitude for the duration. One man had a heart to lead family groups on missionary trips overseas but continued in his job as Children's Pastor for months as he planned starting his family mission trip ministry: "The cloud has moved from here and is leading me on. I just don't have the grace to do my job any longer, but I want to leave on the right terms."

For him to stay would mean delaying or suppressing God's directions within, which would have made him more miserable and unfulfilled, though he loved the families he served. It was too bad he wasn't given the resources to develop that ministry within the pyramid he worked, for it would have been a blessing to many.

I looked back over years of experiences in various church settings and observed that those with entrepreneurial skill, or risk takers, were willing to leave the pyramid they were in to either attend somewhere else, or start up their own ministry.

I saw this pattern repeatedly; whether it was the woman who wanted to start her own after school outreach to children but someone told her no or the children's pastor who wanted to expand the scope of that department but was denied, or the man longing to create TV shows and movies for Christians but was not given the resources to do so at his church, to hundreds in between. Over the years I've seen many who were convinced they'd heard from God and were brave enough to move outside their current pyramid to do what God was leading them to do.

When people with that kind of drive and vision leave a pyramid, it leaves the mediocre and the maintainers to stay within the pyramid, thus weakening the structure as a whole. Frustrated pastors who have the heart but not the gift to head up a church, evangelists who can't make it on the itinerant circuit, people at a season of life they just want a steady job and are willing to do whatever is required as long as it's working for God, and more. They are fine people with hearts of gold, but they may not be gifted with the kind of drive and vision that can take that church department to the next higher level. However, they can maintain what is there and work within the system, and a pastor in a pyramid system needs these valuable people.

They fit well within the pyramid because the pastor needs people who won't challenge him with the real issues that could better the organization. For the sake of peace within the pyramid the pastor doesn't want to spend all his time keeping people in line. Like Moses, he doesn't need a rebellion like Korah's, but rather needs people who will do what they are told and be loyal and consistent. One pastor told me he would take mediocre any day over someone with drive and ambition, because that furthers the vision of the church and makes his job easier. And now understanding the pyramid, I can't blame him.

Eventually an organization can become so thin it has difficulty maintaining itself because the creative spirit has moved on. Thus, the control from above becomes more severe over time, because the basic competence level of the staff is lowered as they become afraid to make a decision without getting someone's approval above them. This creates a bottle neck at the desk of the pastor further enhancing the culture of micromanagement.

I can look over many organizations and see how the Lord has moved people with a higher call and purpose out of these ministries, but then I wonder what could have been, had those people been empowered to move into their call with the resources of the whole ministry to help.

A New Program is the Answer!

What I observed in some churches was that it seemed because all attention is directed to the top man or woman and they feel pressure to keep the church moving on, they must continually put new projects before the people to demonstrate 'God is blessing' the ministry. Pastors think that the answer to growing their church is a new building, or some other project like starting a bus outreach, thus lowering themselves to become in effect, a cheerleader in front of their congregation on behalf of the new offensive.

As a pastor and I talked over lunch he shared the big thing in his area was what was being called by pastors, 'the parking lot anointing.' It seemed that one church decided to raise money to pave over their gravel parking lot, and then when their attendance jumped due to the ease and convenience afforded, other pastors started feeling led of the Lord and had the 'parking lot anointing' come on them. Soon many churches in the area were raising money to pave over their gravel parking lots with competition to have the best access and convenience.

The added benefit of this sort of behavior is that it keeps extra money flowing into the church and people talking. But if this is pushed too much the people will tire of always having some project to fund, yet pyramids don't often stop to just maintain a program.

If the project isn't something like a parking lot that requires no real maintenance for years to come then the funding drive has a clear start and finish. If the drive is for a building or ongoing outreach program there will be continued funds needed once the initial effort is complete.

As a result each of these types of programs saps money away from the general fund, causing a squeeze and requiring ever greater budget increases over the years. In short, they are forced to have drives to underwrite many programs the Lord probably intended to be a short lived and had removed his anointing from long ago.

Like a Wal-Mart, the church has many different departments in which no one department carries the whole of the church, yet the overall presentation to the church goer is that of a church that has everything under its roof. Just as Wal-Mart must have a craft department though it is not a big money maker for them but draws people in, so too a church like this must keep and maintain all its varied programs going strong. Anything else would be seen as a retreat and defeat.

One smaller church I know began a bus ministry with one bus and great enthusiasm and involvement, but after a time the volunteers running the program became weary and resigned their positions. Immediately a call went out to the church for new people to fill in, and with limited success, the program continued, though at a much smaller scale, using a smaller 15 passenger van rather than a school bus. The pastor didn't want to discontinue the program, though the financial partnership within the church had dried up, but by this time the church identified itself with the program in the community. Thus, to discontinue the bus ministry was to suffer a huge defeat for the church (and pastor).

If this pattern occurs over many years, the church or ministry becomes very thin, supported by maintainers (the ones with drive that initiated the program having moved on) and always scrambling for funds.

The Push for Funds, Ultimate Control in a Pyramid

Another trait I saw in many traditional structured churches was heavy Malachi 3 and tithing pressure coupled with condemnation applied to the congregation. The ministry will sometimes share with the congregation that things are tight, but often no mention of a cash crunch is made, just the sudden push for money.

Churches and other ministries are notorious for contracting for construction with the intention of raising money as they go, but when the offerings run short of the budget and construction crews have already performed the work, it is the congregation that gets heavy pressure to come to the rescue of that ministry.

A husband and wife I know were visiting family in California a few years ago when a car crossed the center line and slammed into their car. The wife, who was about 6 1/2 months pregnant spontaneously delivered, but fortunately all 3 of them survived. Finally out of rehabilitation three months later and back in their home, though both husband and wife were in wheelchairs until their lower legs and bones healed completely, they contacted me for help. They had requested a gift of $500 from their church for a mortgage payment but were turned down, but they knew that I knew the Chief Financial Officer, so I offered to help re-submit their request.

They were business owners and faithfully tithed to their church and gave extra offerings besides for at least the 4 years I knew them, so I thought their request was reasonable. I contacted the CFO of the church and told them the situation and that I knew them to be faithful givers, and asked for the $500 for their mortgage. The answer was no.

This couple was deeply hurt and perplexed. They knew the church had a huge budget and surely $500 wouldn't hurt the budget, and couldn't understand why they had been turned down.

Another man on staff at a large church asked for help because their family's air conditioner had broken and it required a new unit, about $1800. They had four young children and were struggling to make ends meet, but served the church faithfully. He was turned down, even when he offered to let them dock his pay each week over a few months until it was paid back, but still the answer was no.

Not only was I saddened by each family's story, but I couldn't understand how the powers that be couldn't understand the issues on two levels, both financially and as a Christian: On a financial level the first man and wife tithed $500 per month over 4 years before he made his request, a total of $24,000, but because of their response he left that church, giving his tithes to another pyramid in town. In the case of the staff member he worked in a department that kept financial records for the church and had saved the church thousands of dollars over the years by his innovations and ideas.

On a purely Christian level I just didn't understand why each respective church wasn't willing to invest in their members. Both seemed clear cut and the right thing to do was obvious, yet they were ignored. The staff member went to another church and actually received a pay raise of many thousands of dollars.

In the pyramid all the money flows to the top and it's all about funding buildings and programs instead of funding people. The focus is on the larger vision instead of the people who make it happen.

As it pertains to the continued push for money, some people will eventually leave the church because of hearing the same broken record over and over. When I asked one leader about this pattern I was told: "If the people would do what they're supposed to do, they wouldn't hear the broken record." I countered, asking "…if you kept hearing the same thing from the people over and over as they leave the church, shouldn't the leaders look to themselves to see what the causes and true issues were to this pattern?"

The push for funds is the result of an obsolete and flawed system, for most church leaders aren't greedy (though some clearly are), but the guilt for its shortcomings is placed on the shoulders of the faithful rather than on the leaders, where it belongs.

Competition

Yet another characteristic of the pyramid, and one of the most obvious, is that of competition. This is very obvious to the man on the street, Christian and non-Christian alike, yet universally denied within the church. Because the traditional structure is based on the person at the top and his or her vision, it becomes a 'kingdom' within itself, competing with other 'kingdoms'. As we saw earlier, if we were to make several pyramids out of cardboard and put them on the floor, we would find that their bases can touch one another, but that is all. Their sides and tops can never touch because of the way they're built. By their design, pyramids are solitary objects, each with it's own 'footprint' and territory in the community.

All over town and in the papers and TV we see various pyramids letting everyone know their unique program, new pastor, special event, witty quote on the billboard out front, or other quality that sets themselves apart from the other pyramids in town.

They advertise 'come worship with us'; 'come see our Easter program' and the like in an effort to draw people in to what they are doing. It is competition with each other plain and simple under the guise of doing it for God.

The ramifications among the pastors are obvious: Jealousy, back stabbing, refusal to fellowship, accusations of sheep stealing, and much more. Ministerial alliance meetings and organizations are filled with pastors in great conflict. They know they must love the pastor of the church across town, but inwardly they are jealous. Others retreat to their pet doctrine or issue and hide behind them as an excuse and refuse to fellowship.

The bases of the pyramids touch, covering a whole city, but the tops do not. The result is a massive flow called 'church hopping' between the pyramid bases, while the tops of the pyramids try to shut the back door. Again, it's the system that is inherently flawed.

Because the leaders in a pyramid are territorial, so will those under them be territorial. The fear and insecurity at the top is huge. Decisions are made out of fear; trying to protect what they have and making sure others don't take away what they've gained.

The Sad Result

The result of focusing on one person at the top to be the font of God's wisdom and word for the people is that the people, not hearing from God themselves, have become weak, malnourished, and unable to feed themselves.

The very thing the church purports to advocate (a strong and vibrant Christianity) is what the nature of a pyramid structure prevents. The pyramid says it is a strong advocate of the family, yet demands attendance and money that take away from family. Many families would be better off to skip a few Sunday or midweek services and take time to do something fun as a family!

The Jethro pyramid actually requires an anemic and helpless populace to maintain itself, and even it's growth is dependent upon the spiritually weak and anemic to fill the pews and their money to fill the coffers.

According to Ralph Neighbour a poll was taken of his city of Houston, Texas. They discovered that 88.5 % of the people do not go to church. That means that only 11.5 % of a population of 4 1/2 million, roughly 500,000 people, goes to church. The pyramid structure has miserably failed the city of Houston.

You can figure this percentage for your own city. Let's look at Tulsa, a city with nearly 400,000 people and about an additional 100,000 in the metro area. There are about five mega churches, with an attendance together totaling maybe 30,000 on any given Sunday. Add in two smaller mega churches totaling 6,000. Add in about five 1,000 member churches. That only comes to 41,000 people. If you add in all the other churches in Tulsa, you may come up with another 20,000 people or so if that, for a total of about 61,000. That's just 12% of the population. Even if you throw in another 20,000 people, that's only about 16% of the city.

I pastored a traditionally styled church in a small town of 3,400 people. There were 22 churches in our town. Our church, the Catholic, and the Methodist church were the 3 largest. Most of the other churches were under 50 people in membership, most hovering around 20. Adding them all up, we managed only about 700 people in church on Sundays. That's about 19% of the population. It doesn't matter what size the town, the pyramid structure has failed.

I don't fault the men and women at the top of their structures, they are just doing church the way they've been taught, though it isn't really the pattern the New Testament describes. Examining the examples above shows quite clearly that the pyramid structure that began in 313AD and solidified in 495AD has failed miserably.

This old, manmade structure is the chief reason the church has become nearly irrelevant in society. It keeps people from flowing the way the Lord designed them, relegating to organizations the duties of 'true religion', visiting the sick, the imprisoned, feeding the hungry, discipling of believers and such, instead of empowering individuals, as the Bible teaches us.

The Conclusion

The conclusion to be drawn is that the pyramid structure provides program or structure based relationships, rather than what I've been calling for years, **Relationship Based Christianity**, touching people where they live.

The pyramid structure forms a program or other structure and then tries to get people to fill that structure and breathe life into it. Relationship based structure found in house church follows life and only forms a structure to serve the Life, changing the structure as needed. For years in the pyramid I had been a cheerleader trying to get people to participate in programs I helped start or develop, in essence asking them to breathe life into it, whereas I should have been looking for life, and responding in such a way not to corral it, but rather adding just enough (if even needed) structure to facilitate the creation of more life.

Chapter 4

How Jesus Portrayed Church Structure

Out of Context

The whole of our New Testament was written to Christians in house based churches about issues and problems within house based churches and relationships, by apostles and leaders who were members of and helped start and develop house based churches.

When Constantine called Christians out of homes and into the format we have today in the traditional church, understanding the New Testament went from understanding it within the context it was written and intended, to being interpreted through the eyes of those within a pyramid shaped organization, thereby losing sight of the real intentions of the authors.

No where is this contrast seen so vividly as when Jesus taught about his leaders.

A "V", not a Pyramid

Jesus stated that church leaders are at the bottom, with him being the chief cornerstone. If anything, for purposes of this discussion, he presents a shallow V rather than a pyramid, with leaders at the bottom submitting upward to those they serve. This is in contrast to the Jethro model.

In Mark 10: 42–45 Jesus said:

"You know that those who are recognized as governing and are supposed to rule the Gentiles (the nations) lord it over them (ruling with absolute power, holding them in subjection), and their great men exercise authority and dominion over them. But this is not to be so among you: instead,

whoever desires to be great among you must be your servant. And whoever wishes to be most important and first in rank among you must be slave of all." (Mark 10:42–44 AMP)

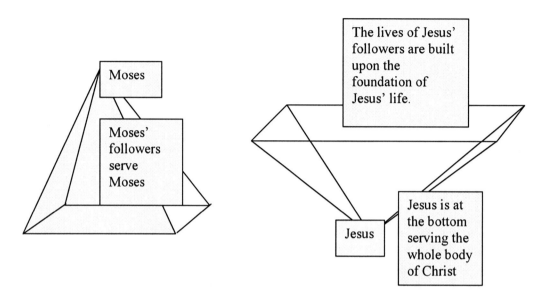

This is contrary to what nearly every Bible school teaches. This is because those schools are teaching the pyramid model, and order among the ranks is required to maintain control of the pyramid. In once sense the pastor at the top of the pyramid can rightly say he is serving his congregation, just as Moses would have rightly said. But serving God in a structure never intended to be the structure of the church means pastors and ministry leaders are working in a structure inherently flawed! It's not the way Jesus stated church leadership should serve: He wants them at the bottom of the building, right next to the Cornerstone, not at the top of a pyramid.

Once I realized that Jethro's pyramid was exactly opposite what Jesus said about leadership, I suddenly understood that because Jethro was helping Moses set up a political structure, the church which was patterned after it could not help but be political in nature. 1700 years of wars, politics, infighting, grappling for control of whole nations and regions of the world, the traditional church is political because of its' structure.

Jesus never intended his (church) leadership to set up a structure that resembled the political organization of Moses, in fact, in the above scripture Jesus makes a point of contrasting the two—the higher rulers exercise authority over the lesser, but it shall not be so among you! The government does rest upon the shoulders of Jesus (Isaiah 9:6); he is at the bottom supporting it, not at the top of a pyramid.

But doesn't Hebrews 13:17 serve as an example of membership being told to submit to leadership?

> **"<u>Obey</u> those that have the rule over you, and submit (yield) yourselves for they watch for your souls, as they much also give account, that they may do it with joy, and not with grief: for that is unprofitable for you." (KJV)**

Vine brings out that this word translated 'obey' is not the word 'obey' (hupakoe) at all. It is the word peitho, which means "to persuade, to win over". He goes on to say,

> **"The 'obedience' suggested is not by submission to authority, but resulting from persuasion."**

He also states: "'Peitho' and the word 'to trust' are closely related.

In other words, the writer of Hebrews is not commanding the people to obey their leadership, he is urging them to be 'persuaded' or 'won over in trust' by the leadership, so leadership (may serve) them with joy.

Understand that <u>the context of the writer of Hebrews is leaders of house churches who are servants first.</u> It is a misappropriation of this passage to pull it from its house church context and have a pastor sitting at the top of a pyramid use it to justify his authority. Yet because people have not put the passage in context much debate and misunderstanding has occurred over this scripture.

If leadership truly does what Jesus told them to do within the context of house church as taught in the New Testament, submitting upwards to those they serve, then those they serve will gladly be persuaded and won over by them. This is because in house church everyone is mutually submitted and accountable.

Jesus' example

Additionally, <u>Jesus' last instruction on the subject of leadership is found in John 13: 4–12 when he washed the feet of the disciples.</u>

Remember that in Mark 10, the disciples are jostling for position and authority, trying to establish their own territory to rule over because all they know is the Jethro pyramid. One wanted to sit on the right of Jesus in his throne and the other wanted to sit on the left—and the others were jealous because James and John (and their mom) had the boldness to ask such a thing, not because they didn't have the same, albeit unspoken ambition! In the context they understood up to that point, in essence one was asking to be Aaron and one wanted to be Joshua, right next to 'Moses' at the top.

If you've seen similar jostling for position in traditional churches it's a sure sign that church is organized as a Jethro pyramid—a political organization.

Jesus told them their hearts were wrong, and the true leadership that comes from God submits to those they serve. He emphasized his point yet again, by performing the most menial task in those days, washing feet. My main exercise is walking along our country roads where we live. When the weather is warm I wear a pair of good leather sandals, and average 5 miles a day. When I get back home my feet and sandals are covered with dust and I have tiny pebbles in my shoes and stuck to the sweat of my feet. The other day after walking I immediately picked up the garden hose and washed out the garage. Some of the spray fell on my feet and it felt good, so I just poured the flow of the hose directly on both my feet, it felt cool and refreshing, and immediately my whole body and mind was refreshed and relaxed.

When Jesus washed the feet of the disciples he was not only serving them by washing off their feet, but indicating that proper servant-based leadership will have the effect of refreshing those served.

That Jesus' last instruction on leadership was washing the feet of his disciples emphasizes his point from Mark 10 that leadership serves, rather than gets served.

The Building of God

The rest of the NT agrees with Jesus. I Cor 3: 10–11 states that Jesus is the foundation and Paul, as an apostle, helped lay the foundation (of Jesus) in the lives of the Corinthians. The very walls of heaven have as its <u>foundation</u>, the lives of the apostles (Rev 21: 14).

Jesus presents leadership being on the bottom of the real church, its people, serving upwards to them. Again we remember the words of Paul in Ephesians 2:20–22:

> **"And are built upon the foundation of the apostles and prophets, Jesus Christ himself being the chief corner stone; In whom all the building fitly framed together grows into a holy temple in the Lord: In whom you also are built together for a habitation of God through the Spirit." (KJV)**

Members of the body of Christ who serve no one, but are only 'consumers' fill this level				
Various ministry and service gifts on this level	Other 5-fold ministry gifts			
Jesus, the Cornerstone of the Temple of God.	Apostles and Prophets			

The Living Temple of God

"For no other foundation can anyone lay than that which is (already) laid, which is Jesus Christ (the Messiah, the Anointed One)." I Cor 3:11 AMP

"And the wall of the city had twelve foundation (stones), and on them the twelve names of the twelve apostles of the Lamb." (Rev 21:14 AMP)

Moses sat at the top looking down at rulers over 1,000s, 100s, 50s and 10s. Jesus said his leadership is at the bottom serving and supporting the rest of the structure. Which structure is better suited for the Holy Spirit to flow through?

Consider the work of the foundation. Foundations serve the rest of the building that rests upon it. When building a house the foundation must first be set and all the weight of the rest of the building rests upon that foundation. In the part of the country where I live, Tulsa, Oklahoma, there is big business in foundation repair.

The soil is largely made of clay that absorbs and holds water, or dries and cracks in drought. Many foundations crack and settle as the soil beneath expands and contracts. For this reason, though Tulsa is in the middle of tornado alley, few homes are able to have a basement because of the soil.

The foundations of each house must be exactly constructed lest the whole house later fall apart due to the surrounding environment. If the foundation isn't right the rest of the building won't be plumb and square, doors will be ajar and walls will crack. The pyramid doesn't have a scriptural foundation, thus it is filled with cracks and imperfections that make it inefficient and undesirable to those who look upon it.

Jesus is the foundation stone of his living temple—the people. A foundation stone, when using stone blocks, must be set the firmest and absolutely true. From that one corner stone the rest of the walls are built, and they must be built straight and level in line with the cornerstone. Jesus is that cornerstone, with the apostles and the '5 fold' right next to him.

Promotion is downward to greater service

Using the previous illustration showing Jesus at the very bottom and members of the body of Christ who are 'consumers' only at the top, we can see that promotion in God is downward to greater service, greater opportunity to lay down one's life for those served, following Jesus' example.

Let's look at the life of Philip, called the Evangelist in Acts 21:8, about the year 60AD. However some 27 years earlier in 33AD Philip is just a member of the body of Christ in Jerusalem with no involvement in any ministry mentioned.

At that time the church was still exclusively in Jerusalem and had a feeding ministry that cared for widows who had no other means of support. Soon prejudice and bias reared its ugly head and the Greek women felt they were being discriminated against in the daily meal schedule. It is unclear who is running the food ministry at that point, but the apostles called everyone together and said "it's not right that we should leave the word of God and serve tables" (to run it properly) (Acts 6:2).

They told the people to choose seven good men who could be appointed to run the food ministry. One of the seven was a man named Steven, and another was Philip. These men came from the congregation with no previous ministry experience mentioned, and were promoted downward to prepare and serve meals to widows with no family or other support, among the lowest class in that day and age.

I should mention that with this promotion downward it was said of Stephen:

"And Stephen, full of faith and power, did great wonders and miracles among the people." (Acts 6:8 KJV)

There is a connection between the level of service and the anointing for ministry gifts in a person's life, as evidenced first and foremost by Jesus' life and ministry of course. Many people want to have signs and wonders follow them, but they don't understand that it requires promotion downward to greater service as the price of admission. Because they were raised in the pyramid system they think having great signs and wonders means more notoriety for themselves and a life of luxury, building a name and ministry following, but from a scriptural standpoint the opposite is true. Steven went from a member of the congregation to waiting tables to martyrdom in short order.

Philip evidently served the recipients of the food ministry well, but there was something larger stirring in his heart; he wanted to reach the unreached. Though thrilled to be chosen from the mass of believers to help serve in the food ministry, his heart was to tell the unsaved about Jesus. The next time we see him mentioned is in Acts 8:5:

"Philip (the deacon, not the apostle) went down to the city of Samaria and proclaimed the Christ (the Messiah) to them (the people); And great crowds of people with one accord listened to and heeded what was said by Philip, as they heard him and watched the miracles and wonders which he kept performing (from time to time). For foul spirits came out of many who were possessed by them, screaming and shouting with a loud voice, and many who were suffering from palsy or were crippled were restored to health. And there was great rejoicing in that city." (Acts 8:5–8 AMP)

Thus we see the progression downward: Philip goes from a member of the congregation to cooking food and waiting tables in the food ministry. Then he goes to Samaria, a town familiar with prejudice and bias because the Jewish culture hated the Samaritans, and preached Jesus with signs and wonders following.

He is mentioned again later in this chapter as having an angel speak to him telling him to start walking along the desert road to Gaza, where he first sees and is then told by the Holy Spirit to preach to an Ethiopian Eunuch. After ministering salvation and baptism to the Eunuch the text says:

"And when they came up out of the water, the Spirit of the Lord (suddenly) caught away Philip; and the eunuch saw him no more, and he went on his way rejoicing. But Philip was found at Azotus and passing on he preached the good news (Gospel) to all the towns until he reached Caesarea." (Acts 8:39–40 AMP)

Evidently Philip chose to live in Caesarea for that is where we next find him 27 years later when Acts 21: 8 says:

"On the morrow we left there and came to Caesarea; and we went into the house of Philip the evangelist, who was one of the Seven (first deacons), and stayed with him."

Philip started "up" as a member of the congregation having dreams and a heart to serve the people, promoted downward to cooking food and waiting tables, and promoted downward still to become an evangelist near the bottom, his life long call and ministry.

Truly promotion in the New Testament structure is downward to greater service, not upward in a pyramid like the civil government of Jethro and Moses.

Enter the family (again)

Before Constantine called Christians out of their homes the church was winning the Roman Empire one household at a time. Disciples of Jesus were in all walks of life, all careers, all socio-economic levels. By leadership serving those they served from the homes outward, the whole culture changed.

Just as the husband is commanded in Ephesians 5:25 to give his life for his wife as Christ did for the church, so too from the family extend outreaching arms to neighbors, eager to share the secret of walking through life with God at your side. From that family the outflow continues, until (over the course of 3 centuries) the whole Empire was changed. It is not by accident that Acts 21: 9 mentions that Philip had four teenage daughters who were known for the gift of prophecy. He served his family first and then outward to others, keeping everything in the right order and perspective.

The most non-political structure on earth is the family and home. Each member is recognized and valued as an individually gifted and unique person, and the leadership (parents) in the home is to help develop the children therein by mentoring and guiding them through life. What a beautiful picture of the discipleship process, for scripture presents striking parallels between spiritual growth and physical growth.

> **"Like newborn babies you should crave (thirst for, earnestly desire) the pure (unadulterated) spiritual milk, that by it you may be nurtured and grow unto (completed) salvation." (I Peter 2:2 AMP)**

> **"So then, we may no longer be children...rather let our lives lovingly express truth...let us grow up in every way and in all things into Him..." (Eph 4:14–15 AMP)**

> **"However brethren, I cold not talk to you as to spiritual, but as to non-spiritual...as to mere infants...I fed you with milk, not solid food, for you were not yet strong enough to be ready for it; but even yet you are not strong enough...for you are still (unspiritual),...for as long as there are envying and jealousy and wrangling and factions among you, are you not unspiritual..." (I Cor 1–3 AMP)**

I began to see that Jesus intended the church to be much like a well balanced home, a place of nurturing and security and love, rather than a political structure like the pyramid.

Consider the Contrast

The contrast between what Jesus instructed and the Jethro pyramid is stark. Clearly they are opposites, yet God moves through both so I don't want the reader to get the idea I'm against the pyramid just because of my examination of its flaws. One structure is the way Jesus and the disciples did 'church' and the context of the whole of the New Testament; while the other is man-made, having been around for only the last 1700 years, yet God has used and is using both ways of "doing" church.

The Jethro pyramid demands allegiance to one leader based on the job to do whereas Jesus stated leaders submit to those they serve, obviously based on giftings and relationship of service.

Suddenly I realized that house church was not the abnormal, the traditional church was abnormal. House church was the normal way of doing church and the traditional pyramid was man's invention. The book of Acts is normal Christianity, what I see around me in the traditional church is not normal Christianity.

It suddenly made sense. Over the years I've heard of traditionally structured churches struggling to set up a council of elders, the removal of a single man as pastor, instead to be ruled by a group of men. In their effort to be more Biblical they were trying to take elements of Jesus' V structure and make it work in the pyramid—and that's why they failed.

In fact, as I mentally reviewed all the instances where I'd seen that type of thing tried, they all failed. Why? Because the ramifications of adhering to Jesus instructions are not a restructuring of the pyramid, they are the destruction of the pyramid. A pastor who wishes to adapt to a house church format must give away his church, empower leaders, and then the church will actually grow by the making of disciples, rather than through the assimilation of other church's members into itself. The senior pastor becomes what Paul called 'an elder who serves well and is worthy of double honor…for you shall not muzzle the ox.' (I Tim 5:17–18) In other words, Paul said there are times when leaders should draw a paycheck from the network of (house) churches they serve. Such is the Biblical model.

Consider that all your Christian life you have been reading Matthew through The Revelation, maybe not understanding that these books were originally letters written to people meeting in living rooms all over the Roman Empire.

If you are like me, you didn't understand the context or pulled verses from passages and tried to fit them into the pyramid structure of church as we've known it, having to offer explanations that didn't quite fit but you didn't know exactly why. House church is the only format I've found in which the Bible truly is the manual in how to do church. Whole bookstore shelves and many a pastor's library are filled with books on how to do church, all based on the pyramid model, thus needing that volume of material to help make it work. But house church started in the Garden of Eden and has continued throughout man's history, and the whole of the NT was written within that context. How wonderful to be fully in synch with Jesus and the way he portrayed church to be!

Again, keep in mind that God follows his Genesis command and seeks to fill whatever structure man will give him, so I want to reiterate that God can and does flow through the pyramid. However, the point is that doing church as Jesus and the apostles practiced it is the highest and best way for God to flow among his people, and for those people to grow in Christ.

Chapter 5

Ekklesia

I began reexamining 'church' as a word and concept when I realized the pyramid that I knew was opposite of what Jesus actually taught and modeled. Surely if what Jesus taught, that 'from the bottom up' leadership served, then there must be a structure given for that method of leadership to flow through.

What did the word 'church' mean to the disciples and first century Christians? I had to start there. There are several words Jesus could have used to signify a gathering together of people who were meeting for the same purpose if that's all he was trying to convey 'church' was. For instance, the word 'paneguris' means "any kind of assembly" (Vine), but he didn't use that word. Jesus could have used 'plethos', which means "a multitude, the whole number" (Vine), or several others, but he didn't.

Jesus used the word 'ekklesia' which is translated 'church'. Ekklesia comes from *ek*, "out of," and *klesis*, "a calling" (Vine). It means literally then, "a calling out of". But if all we understood was "a calling out of" we still wouldn't understand why Jesus chose that particular word. The trouble is that nearly all the teaching and writing about 'ekklesia' that is out there is limited to the linguistically literal interpretation of the word as stated above and not the word set in the context of Jesus and his disciples and their understanding of the application of that word. In that setting the meaning of ekklesia goes way beyond merely being called out of.

What did Jesus' disciples understand that word to be when they heard it? What was its use in that day and age and did it convey anything beyond just a group of people called out? We must remember that until its first use in Matthew 16:18, Jesus had never used that word to describe his followers.

"Then he asked them, "Who do you think I am?" Simon Peter answered, "The Christ, the Messiah, the Son of the living God." "Then Jesus answered him, Blessed—happy, fortunate and to be envied—are you

Simon Bar-Jonah, for flesh and blood (men) have not revealed this to you, but My Father Who is in heaven. And I tell you, you are Peter (Petros, a piece of rock), and on this rock (Petra, a huge rock like Gibraltar) I will build My <u>church</u> (ekklesia), and the gates of Hades (the powers of the infernal region) shall not overpower it—or be strong to its detriment, or hold out against it." (Mt 16:15–18 AMP)

The word 'ekklesia' was used to signify a very specific type of meeting, and not just any type of meeting, and this is what the disciples heard it to be straight from the lips of Jesus. Ekklesia was used among the Greeks as a meeting of the citizens of a city-state who were called and gathered to conduct the business of that city-state. Vine says: "…was used among the Greeks of a body of citizens "gathered" to discuss the affairs of state…"

The Greeks used to be a nation of individual city-states, similar in some respects to feudal Europe with castles dotting the countryside controlling the lands in the area, each little kingdom a world of its own. When any of the Greek city-states had business to conduct, they would call an ekklesia—a church, which was a gathering of its citizens for the purpose of conducting the business of the kingdom.

Thus the first use of 'called out' is not called out of the world, but rather called out to conduct the business of the kingdom.

When Peter responded that Jesus was the Christ, the Son of the living God, Jesus said that flesh and blood had not revealed this to him, rather the Father (through the Holy Spirit). He then said Peter was a stone, but upon this ROCK he would build his gathering of citizens who would meet to conduct the affairs of the kingdom.

What is the rock we must ask? The rock is not Peter, for Jesus clearly said he was merely a petros, a stone. The Petra, the Rock, is the revelation that Jesus is the Christ, the Son of the Living God, revealed by God, and upon THIS massive rock like Gibraltar Jesus would build his gathering of citizens to conduct the business of the kingdom.

The whole kingdom of heaven, and the church/ekklesia itself is built upon the revelation that Jesus is not just another prophet, not just another holy man, each person in the kingdom has had a revelation from God through the Holy Spirit that Jesus is the Christ, the Son of the living God. This is the rock the gathering of citizens is built upon!

Church therefore is not a building, rather a meeting for the purpose of conducting the business of the kingdom by citizens of that kingdom.

As I studied this fact I realized that the pyramid—the standard Sunday morning in a traditional church—was not structured in a way to facilitate the receiving of revelation, nor set up to conduct the business of the kingdom. Or perhaps I should say, its' structure limits the amount of revelation and limits the business conducted in a typical meeting to a designated person pre-determined to give forth his or her revelation in a predetermined format.

I came to realize that if I thought meeting with a bunch of near-strangers or even friends in an auditorium for 4 songs, a plea for money, and a 40 minute sermon was all there was to conducting the business of the kingdom, I was sorely mistaken!

The intent of Jesus using this word to signify a gathering of citizens to conduct the business of the kingdom is further reinforced when he tells them that the 'gates of hell' will not prevail against it.

In Jesus' time, as in Old Testament times, the gates of a city represented the place of power and authority. It was at the gate of the city that Boaz met with the elders of the city to attain the right to marry Ruth. It was at the gate of the city that Absalom sat and made judgments, undermining his father King David. It was the gate of Gaza Samson carried off on his back, and Job, remembering his former glory days spoke of his place among the nobles at the gates of the city. The gates of a city are where the business of that city (or kingdom) takes place.

Jesus paints a picture of two kingdoms at odds, but the gathering of his citizens who are founded upon divine revelation that he is the Christ will in fact prevail against the leadership of the kingdom of hell.

Suddenly I understood the importance of revelation from God in a new way. Paul said in I Corinthians 14:6 that his coming to them wouldn't benefit them unless he had either revelation, or knowledge (of God) or prophesying (spoken revelation to someone) or teaching (knowledge gained by revelation). He went on to say that when they come together someone in the meeting may have a revelation or the gifts of the Spirit may move (both based on revelation). Certainly the Charismatic gifts are all about revelation for people—whether healing or words of knowledge or miracles, it's all about bringing the revelation that Jesus is the Christ and his ministry to people.

As I thought back over my life I realized that I had made no major decision until and unless there was a peace in my spirit, or a 'good witness', or a word from the Lord—in other words, some form of revelation from the Lord that gave me the sense I was in His perfect will. The kingdom operates on revelation from the Father through the Holy Spirit, and it is those revelations around which our lives pivot.

I realized one reason I was feeling so disconnected from Sunday morning was that there was little real revelation from heaven—the pyramid was stuck in a format that hadn't changed in 1,700 years. In the traditional church the only revelation expected is from the pastor's sermon. Yet the meaning of Jesus' use of ekklesia in Matthew's gospel revolves around revelation given by heaven for the purpose of conducting battle against the enemy's gates as it pertains to the lives of people. How could the business of the kingdom be conducted in a pyramid?

Jesus went on to say in Matthew 16:19:

"I will give you the keys of the kingdom of heaven, and whatever you bind—that is declare to be improper and unlawful—on earth must be already bound in heaven; and whatever you loose on earth—declare lawful—must be what is already loosed in heaven." (AMP)

Jesus is clearly talking about a gathering of people in his kingdom meeting to do the business of the kingdom and taking the battle to the enemy kingdom based on their revelation from God.

The term binding and loosing as Jesus used them have to do with the gathering of citizens giving their stamp of approval or not. In the same way today we would go to the courthouse—no longer using the gates of the city to meet the city council—to receive licensing or permits, Jesus was telling them the ekklesia had the authority to govern.

Additionally, the Amplified Version translates the passage to say:

"whatever you (declare to be unlawful) must be <u>already bound in heaven</u>...whatever you loose...must be what is <u>already loosed in heaven</u>."

<u>This would indicate a very close working relationship between heaven and the ekklesia, with heaven directing by revelation instructions to its' members.</u>

This can only be accomplished in a setting that allows revelation to flow—to hear what heaven is saying through the gifts within the ekklesia, and then taking the battle to the enemy's leadership.

If we read the passage straight through its meaning within the context it was intended becomes clear:

"upon this Rock of revelation from the Father I will build my gathering of citizens who are meeting to conduct the business of the kingdom, and the leadership of hell will not prevail against it. I will give you the keys of the kingdom and whatever heaven reveals to you that isn't lawful, it won't be lawful, and whatever heaven reveals is lawful, you will allow it to be lawful, (and the leadership of hell will not be able to stand against it...)"

In practice this occurs when someone has (for example but not limited to) a prophecy—a word of edification, exhortation, or comfort for someone. Sometimes heaven reveals to someone a word of knowledge about someone or an issue they should pray for, maybe even something or someone on a national level. It happens when the Lord lays it on someone's heart to bring a bag of groceries to a friend in need...whatever heaven reveals it is for the purpose of directing the ekklesia to conduct the business of the kingdom, and the leadership of hell will not prevail against that revelation.

Clearly the intent of the revelation is not limited to the singular salvation experience of realizing Jesus is the Christ, but ongoing, day to day revelation that enables the ekklesia to conduct the business of the kingdom.

Jesus was telling his disciples that when his people came together they were to do so with the intent of hearing from heaven. He was telling them that revelation from heaven was the purpose and means by which the gathering would prevail against the leadership of the enemy. Thus the first priority of (house) church is to establish an atmosphere in which God can reveal what he wants when he wants, and how he wants.

Because the ekklesia conducts its business based on ongoing revelation flowing from heaven, the will of the Father in people's lives is seen on the earth. "Thy kingdom come, thy will be done on earth as it is in heaven" becomes a reality, one person at a time!

The writers of the New Testament did not address their letters to the leadership of a church; they addressed them to the whole gathering of citizens of the kingdom.

Not one letter in the NT was written to the "elders of the church at..." Paul simply wrote 'to the **church (ekklesia)** at _____'. He didn't write, "To the **leadership** at _____".

"Paul...to all that be in Rome, beloved of God..." (Rom 1:1, 7)

"Paul…to the church of God which is at Corinth…" (I Cor 1:1–2)

"Paul…to the church of God which is at Corinth…" (II Cor 1:1)

"Paul…to the churches of Galatia…" (Gal 1:1–2)

"Paul…to the saints which are at Ephesus…" (Eph 1:1)

"Paul…to all the saints in Christ Jesus which are at Philippi with the bishops and deacons" (Phil 1:1) Here in his warmest letter he merely includes leadership in his greetings, but actually addresses the letter "to all the saints."

"Paul…to the saints and faithful brethren at Colossae…" (Col 1:1)

"Paul…to the church of the Thessalonians…" (I Thess 1:1)

"Paul…to the church of the Thessalonians…" (II Thess 1:1) (all above KJV)

The two letters to Timothy, as well as the one to Titus and Philemon were to individuals rather than the whole body.

Paul addressed the whole church in his general epistles rather than leadership because they all are to participate in the business of the kingdom. Any of them could receive revelation. This is exactly opposite the pyramid whose services are designed to keep people from participating (except for the leaders) and requires only the top person and highest ranking overseers to make decisions. This is one reason Paul told the church at Corinth who had two brothers suing each other to choose those they esteemed least and let them judge. (I Cor 6:1–4) He didn't tell leadership to handle it, he told the body to handle it.

The next question must be, "If he expected everyone to be involved, then what is the business of the kingdom?" Actually, the answer stares us in the face in the Great Commission:

> **"...All authority—all power of rule—in heaven and on earth has been given to Me. <u>Go then and make disciples of all the nations</u>, baptizing them into the name of the Father and of the Son and of the Holy Spirit; <u>Teaching them to observe everything that I have commanded you</u>..." (Mt 28:18–20—AMP)**

Clearly, the business of the kingdom Jesus was talking about was the making of disciples. It is within this context that we take the battle to the enemy's gates, freeing the oppressed and healing the hurting. If our ekklesia isn't about the discipleship process then we aren't truly fulfilling the purpose of the ekklesia.

As I examined the traditional churches around me, especially the megachurches, suddenly an apparent incongruity made sense. God was moving more in the small groups than he was on Sunday morning. People were actually seeing breakthroughs in the living rooms of people throughout the city and lives were being changed in the small groups. Now I understood why—the Holy Spirit flows when the ekklesia is actually doing what it was designed to do—and it was designed to conduct the business of the kingdom, which is furthering the discipleship process.

I noticed something else, and that is that in the Great Commission (or anywhere else) Jesus never said anything about getting people born again. His private conversation with Nicodemus about how a person enters the kingdom was just that—a private explanation to 1 man, not instructions to the disciples.

He said to make disciples by teaching them. It goes without saying that a person will be born again, but it became clear to me why we in the west have put all the emphasis on getting a person to pray that prayer of salvation with us.

It has to do with relationships. Getting a person 'born again' by just praying a prayer with us or raising their hand in a meeting and repeating a prayer removes any necessity of us having a relationship (and thereby commitment) to that person. We can report that we got someone born again, but we can do so without even knowing their name!

Consider the 12 disciples. Peter and Andrew were brothers, who were in the fishing business with two other brothers, James and John. (Luke 5:10) That means that 1/3 of the 12 were related or in business together. Then John 1:44–49 records that Philip, from the same town as Peter and Andrew and probably a fisherman as well, found Jesus and went to get his friend Nathanael to tell him they'd found the

Messiah. So at least 1/2 of the original 12 were friends, with 4 of those 6 in business together.

One of the Hebrew words for 'instruct' is the word, "lamad". Lamad is the combination of hearing and doing, not making a distinction between the two. It's used in I Chronicles 25:7, listed below in both the Amplified and KJV:

> **"So the number of them (who led the remainder of the 3,000, with their kinsmen who were <u>specially trained</u> (lamad) in songs for the Lord, all who were talented singers, was 288." (AMP)**

> **"So the number of them, with their brethren that <u>were instructed</u> in the songs of the Lord, even all that were cunning, was 288." (KJV)**

The arts require a high level of devotion and commitment to ongoing instruction and training, and thus provide a perfect example of both instruction and the application of that instruction. A person must do more than just read the notes on a page; they must practice the application of those notes over and over and over again.

It is this concept that explains why Jesus both taught the disciples and lived with them for three and a half years. Mark 4:34 says that Jesus spoke to the people in parables, but when he was alone with the disciples he explained them more fully in private.

The New Testament equivalent in concept is the word 'disciple'. Vine's Dictionary of New Testament Words says this of the word 'disciple':

> **"Lit., a learner (from manthano, to learn, from a root math-, indicating <u>thought accompanied by endeavor</u>. A disciple was not only a pupil, but an adherent; hence they are spoken of as imitators of their teacher."**

This word is also translated 'instructed' in Matthew 13:52:

> **"He said to them, Therefore every teacher and interpreter of the Sacred Writings who <u>has been instructed</u> about and trained for the kingdom of heaven and has become a disciple is like a householder who brings forth out of his storehouse treasure that is new and (treasure that is) old (the fresh as well as the familiar)." (AMP)**

Notice that in New Testament thought there is no separation between the thought or concept and the application of that concept, again explaining why Jesus lived with his disciples rather than just appoint a certain time and place they'd all meet each day.

In our western or Greek thought we separate the hearing from the doing. Our Christian meetings are filled with people who go to see the TV teacher when he or she is in town to be entertained, not because they intend to apply what they hear. They go because someone is funny or they are a good teacher, but they can also remain anonymous while gaining food for thought without relationships that require accountability and growth. That person can have a good time and fill their Bible with notes, and then promptly forget what they heard. But they'll remember it was a good time.

That isn't to say God doesn't bless and impart things to his people during those meetings, but I have observed many who go merely because it's a good time and they have nothing else to do. "Are you going to see ___?" fills the evening agenda as easily as a dinner and movie, its entertainment to many, something to do.

Paul experienced this in Athens, Greece on Mars Hill, and promptly left because they just wanted to hear the teaching but had no intention of applying it:

> **"Now when they had heard (that there had been) a resurrection from the dead, some scoffed; but others said, We will hear you again about this matter. So Paul went out from among them." (Acts 17:32–33—AMP)**

Because the West is trained in Greek thought of separating the thought from the action rather than the Oriental thought of considering them one, Christianity in the West is filled with hearers instead of hearers and doers. This is why the Pyramid structure of the last 1700 years arose and has flourished as it has in the west. Europe and the West consider it part of their culture to go and hear someone speak truths and good ideas, but applying those ideas are a personal choice and freedom to do so or not.

One of the main reasons the house church concept of the New Testament flourished originally was the Hebrew and Oriental emphasis on family, elders, community, mutually accountable relationships, and the doing of what you are instructed. As the church became more and more Gentile over the next 2 centuries and thus more and more European, Greek thought took over. It was at this point in history Constantine called Christians out of homes and into auditoriums, and the two (Greek thought and the auditorium) melded perfectly with one another.

The house church movement flourishes once again most successfully in the Orient and East because they have the Biblical model of not separating the thought from the action. A friend of mine made a trip to India and noted the close knit relationships among the Christians there and commented to his host about the difference between American and Indian Christianity. His host replied:

> **"You Americans preach a different gospel than we do in India. You tell people if you receive Jesus as your Lord you will be healed, you will be made rich, you will have relationships healed. In India we tell them if they receive Jesus as Lord you may lose your health, you may lose your possessions; you may lose your family, you may lose your life."**

We marvel at the persecution suffered by Christian leaders in China and the East in general, including behind the Veil of Islam, and wonder how they can suffer so. The answer is that they are ready to die the moment they make Jesus Lord of their lives. They understand the context of the New Testament and that there is no separation between the teaching and the application. To receive Jesus means being conformed to his image, even death at the hands of persecutors. To many in the west, conforming the body means to cut back on sweets or begin an exercise program or watch what we say and we think we've made progress as a disciple.

Certainly any study of the Gospels reveals a close knit group of men and women all interconnected by family and business during the ministry of Jesus as well as throughout the whole book of Acts. I also remembered that Barnabus, the son of comfort of Acts 4:36, was the one who got to know the new disciple Paul from his time at Damascus, and when all the apostles were afraid of Paul, Barnabus introduced him to them. (Acts 9:27)

Clearly the precedent set forth in disciple making is first and foremost to move within one's own sphere of influence with people we already know or have something in common with, rather than in anonymous and impersonal mass meetings and the raising of a hand. House church is about walking through life together with others who meet in the same living room(s) each week and often outside those meetings. Teaching is more than a message; it's a process of learning by observing and then applying those truths into your own life. It's not coaching or other type of employer/employee relationship, rather its friendship and fathering, mothering and parenting others as they learn to apply God's word and ways into their lives.

A first time mother and her husband couldn't figure out why their young son kept crying through the night. To them he seemed comfortable in his little crib, but still he cried. It was a new friend and mother of 4 who came alongside and lovingly told the young mother that her baby was cold. To the new parents they thought their son was warm enough, but they didn't realize that baby who had spent 9 months in a 98.6 degree womb took some time to get his body adjusted to 72 degree room temperature. It wasn't a book that taught that mother, it was knowledge through a friend which was an impartation mere words on a page could never convey.

A young man was having problems with internet pornography and confided in an older man in his house church. The older man walked the young man through a lifetime's experience of resisting and successfully overcoming temptations, and then set up a means of accountability that enabled the young man to be set free from that sin.

Both these cases illustrate how people need more than just teaching from the Bible; they need someone to walk them through the process of how to apply that Word into their lives. The house church is just such a format, the format Jesus advocated and the apostles propagated.

Nobody can teach another person anything unless that person is willing to receive from the teacher. When Jesus said 'make disciples, teaching them all I commanded you' the inference is that a relationship exists between the two. Suddenly Paul's method of going to synagogues to find people already somewhere close to the same page spiritually makes sense. He was teaching about Jesus from a foundation of commonality with them in the scriptures, seeing who would accept his word and thereby choose to be a disciple of Jesus.

This is not to ignore the work of the evangelist who does preach to strangers as found by our one example in Acts 8 in the person of "Philip the Evangelist". But most of us are not evangelists.

Even his campaign of Acts 8 was to Samaria, a place Jesus had been in John 4, where the woman at the well event occurred. You may recall that the whole place believed on Jesus not only through her words, but because over the two days he stayed with them, he taught them (John 4:40–42). It should also be noted that Acts 8:1 specifically tells us that all the disciples moved out of Jerusalem to Samaria and Judea due to persecution from Saul. So even though he preached to strangers, they were not entirely ignorant of the things of Jesus.

This makes Philip's efforts there a kind of follow up to what Jesus had done, updating the people on what had had transpired since Jesus' time with them, and explaining the faith further, and a huge number responded.

Additionally, when Philip was finished Peter and John came to take the people to the next step, and that wasn't turning them over to the pyramid, rather the establishment of (still more) house based churches in the region. This was easily done because of the huge numbers of believers in the area that had earlier escaped Jerusalem.

The huge open air meetings we know today, while wonderful for their type of setting, are (today) based on the pyramid structure, not requiring any relationship between the speaker and the hearers. Is it any wonder that people have said even Billy Graham's statistics are something like only 5% or so of those converted remain true to the Lord? Praise God for what those meetings do and have done, but the church is growing today around the world through Relationship Based Christianity in homes and villages and the workplace, not in the mega or other traditionally structured churches or their crusades.

The work of the ekklesia is to conduct the business of the kingdom, and that business is the process of discipleship through close knit relationships in which all are mutually accountable, willing to lay down their lives for each other. Based on revelation from heaven for the purpose of helping each other become more Christ-like, the leadership of hell will not be able to stand against it.

Chapter 6

Authority and Honor Based on Gifts, Not "Office"

There was one more concept I had from my upbringing in the pyramid that needed investigation, which was the term 'office' to describe ministry gifts. The contrast is this; in the pyramid it is the office that is respected, in Jesus' structure it is the gift placed in the heart of a person by God that is honored.

In the pyramid it is all about the job that needs doing. A person may be able to do the job, they may be educated and trained in that job, but is that their gift? (Who cares, just do the job). One man moved to a new town with the intention of becoming involved in the adult Sunday school and Bible school of a particular church. Wanting to get to know the work of that church, he attended a Friday night crusade at a housing project and met the pastor. Without waiting to hear what was on this man's heart, the pastor told him he needed to get involved in the bus ministry and passed him off to that department's Director. They were short of volunteers and the pastor and Director were more concerned that they get help than whether it was God's will for the man to help that program, or if he was gifted for that ministry. Such is the pyramid.

The Jethro pyramid doesn't care if your gift is for that stream of ministry; they just want the job done. I was discovering Jesus' way is recognizing the graces he put in his people and giving them a set of relationships with others through which they may flow.

In the pyramid people are interchangeable as long as the job gets done. Want ads tout the job requirements, education requirements, and life experience requirements, but nowhere does it state the employer or church is concerned that you actually have the giftings and heart to do the job. Thus, both churches and businesses are filled with people educated for a job and/or doing a job but whose heart really isn't in it.

Furthermore, churches and businesses are filled with people who really don't like their jobs and the reason they don't like their job is because they have no God given gift for it. That is why there are administrators who have no gift for administration, not having an inborn ability to organize and delegate, making everyone under their authority miserable, even as they are miserable trying to do a job they are trained for but have no natural ability in.

From all that I'd studied about house church in scripture and the way Jesus and Paul ministered and chose ministry companions; I saw that it was based on heart and giftings, pulling the potential from within people as they matured in Christ rather than just trying to fill a job vacancy.

You may not think of Peter's gift as a fisherman being able to directly flow into being an apostle, but look again. Luke 5:10 says that Peter, James and John were partners in the fishing business, and they had at least 2 boats. Peter is so often portrayed as rough and uneducated, more along the lines of a high school graduate car mechanic than a Harvard trained MBA high in a corporate structure, that we overlook that he owned his own business along with 2 partners.

In the first century fishing business that meant he had the boats, nets, and other equipment to care for, marketing their catch, negotiating a price for their catch, balancing the books and payroll, and so forth. Peter was an entrepreneur capable of juggling many tasks at once while coordinating a division of labor between his partners and supporting at least 3 families.

Jesus just put that gift in another structure to flow through. Peter's ability to partner with others in the fishing business, the boat, nets, hard work, and marketing of the catch was the same set of gifts used as an apostle starting churches, traveling long and hard, writing, and evangelizing his people. (the same could be said of James and John, Peter's fishing and business partners)

Gift or Office?

One of the areas I studied was the 'apostolic movement' which in some circles is quite large. People are running around calling themselves apostles, glorifying the 'office' of apostle and prophet in particular, and I'm not questioning their call, just how that call functions in their pyramid.

In scripture apostles and prophets (and the other 5-fold) are found at the bottom of Jesus' organization within the context of house church, not at the top of pyramids. Apostles planted churches based in homes and helped the discipleship process from the bottom of the Living Temple, next to the Cornerstone. Trying to put an 'apostle' at the top of a pyramid leads to confusion and error. Like washing your feet with your socks on, something just doesn't feel right about it.

I've heard of 'apostles' telling congregations the reason they are rough and appear to be rude is because they are apostles (or prophets), it's part of their office (tell that to Jesus, Peter or Paul). I've heard of apostles ministering once or twice in a (traditional) church and then demand the church pay them a tithe off the offerings from that point forward. Many 'apostles' <u>require</u> members of their network, usually pastors in a traditional pyramid, tithe directly to THEM personally each month.

I've seen some of this style of leadership in action, from TV teachers to 'apostles'. One of them threw a fit in a restaurant because the waitress put the dressing on the salad instead of on the side, reducing her to tears; to yelling and screaming at employees, justifying their actions because their 'office' and gift to the body of Christ makes them that way. I just can't see Jesus acting like that though, can you?

> **My observation is that many 'apostles' are really running nothing more than the pyramid of Jethro, even some who are planting and helping house churches.**

This of course is in complete contrast to the true nature and spirit of the '5-fold', who Jesus said should be at the bottom of the building looking up, not ruling from the top of a pyramid looking down at his or her 'rulers'.

Like the traditional church trying to include elements of Jesus' "V" in the pyramid, putting 'apostles and prophets' at the top won't work. Soon, apostolic organizations that are structured as a pyramid run into financial, personnel, and other problems because they are neither one way nor the other—and a compromise just won't work as well as if those gifts were in the flat or bottom up structure of Jesus' design. But again, God will seek to fill whatever structure man gives him which means the Lord will move to the fullest extent he can in that structure.

Where are the gifts to be used?

In Ephesians 4:8 Paul tells us that Jesus, 'ascended up on high and gave **gifts** unto men', followed by a listing of the 5-fold gifts which are for the perfecting of the saints for the work of the ministry. He did not give offices; he gave gifts, which are functions.

> **The word gift merely describes a <u>function not an office</u>.**

For instance, the word 'apostle' merely means 'sent one'. So the gift of 'sent ones' was given by Jesus for the perfecting of the saints. Their function is to go and start (house) churches and raise up disciples. The word prophet is 'one who speaks forth openly' (Vine) which signifies that gift being one where a person speaks the elements of a divine message.

The word evangelist describes the gift that is 'a messenger of good' (Vine), and the word 'pastor' describes one who 'tends herds or flocks' (Vine). The word teacher merely describes 'one who gives instruction' (Vine).

Similarly, the word 'helps' from I Cor. 12:28 means 'a laying hold of or helping'; 'governments' means 'to guide' (Vine) and so forth. These aren't offices to be honored; they are (merely) functions at the bottom of the Temple of God's people, serving them.

These words which described functions to the people who originally read them in the first century, have through the years been pulled out of the home context and read through the eyes of the pyramid structure and interpreted as offices to be honored, because that's what fits in the pyramid.

These functions are planted within the spirits of men and women when they are created to such an extent that they will not be fulfilled until and unless they are functioning in their respective gifts.

This is true of spiritual gifts as well as intellectual and physical gifts as well. In most uses the words gifts and talents are interchangeable. In the same way a person can operate in the gift of prophecy and the more they flow in that gift the better they become functioning in it, so too does someone with a physical or intellectual gift develop their use and familiarity with their talents/gifts.

Michael Jordan is widely regarded as the best all around basketball player of all time, yet in high school he didn't cause a stir. He had to develop his gift by getting to know it, himself, and becoming familiar with the ways his gift could flow. For instance, when he first played for the Chicago Bulls the nightly newscasts would highlight his high scoring games, yet it was when he learned to pass the ball and spread the scoring around that the Bulls won their championships, thus elevating his gift to the highest level possible.

We already assign honor to people according to their gifts and talents, or functions in the world, but when it comes to church we talk about the 'office' of apostle or 'office' of prophet and our minds go 'tilt'. We speak of someone who "stands in the office of prophet", as if the office is separate from the gift or somehow because it's in church the definitions change. We delight in the singing abilities of the worship team and then turn the microphone over to someone in the 'office' of pastor or teacher.

We have to remember that everything that makes us ourselves comes from God. In Him we live and move and have our being. That means that no matter how we classify the graces we have—gift, talent, 'office'—they are all "functions" and gifts from God.

If I were to tell you that Cary Grant is my favorite actor and Audrey Hepburn my favorite actress (true), you would nod in acknowledgement of their skills and perhaps add your own opinion. I admire their acting gift and ability. If I were to offer the opinion that Celine Dion has one of the most beautiful voices in the world you might agree, but put forth other wonderful singers. There are many God-gifted singers, and we honor them for their gift.

We could go on about photographer Ansel Adams, artists Michelangelo, Rembrandt, or maybe Leonardo DaVinci, all assigned honor according to their gifts. But I encourage you to continue expanding your thoughts outside the 'gift' box. DaVinci was a genius in science as well as painting and other arts. Isn't that gift for science equal to his gift for art? Isn't his talent in painting a gift as much as his genius in science is a gift?

What about Sir Isaac Newton, clearly a believer, he invented Calculus and 'discovered' the law of gravity and other laws of thermodynamics, isn't that ability evidence of God gifting him in those areas?

Have you ever known a true craftsman of wood? Certainly that ability is God given. How about a car mechanic? Have you ever known a man who 'could fix anything' so to speak? What about a seamstress or naturally great cook or baker? Our gifts and talents are all given by God and we need to stop thinking that giftings from God are only in the area of the 5-fold or other spiritual application.

I know a nurse who was in the midst of a midlife crisis at her job in the oil and gas industry. She was successful but very unhappy and she didn't know why. Then she realized she wasn't fulfilled because there was nothing in her that was flowing out to her job. It was just a job. She wasn't what we'd call a strong Christian, but she believed in God. One night late as she was lying in bed with her husband beside her, she was thinking on what to do with her life and heard a voice. "You're going to be a nurse." She was so startled she asked her husband what he said, but he responded that he hadn't said anything.

Then she recognized the voice as the Lord who then said, "You're going to be laid off from your job, but I will pay for your schooling." When she told her husband he asked, "Did God tell you how we were going to get by on one income?" She said that he had not, but she was convinced it would work out.

This was in the early 1980s, when the Tulsa oil industry collapsed, and within 5 days of this experience her boss told her he was going to have to lay her off at the end of the pay period that next week. Two days later, still a bit confused and wondering how she and her husband were going to get by, her boss said he had discovered that due to the industry collapse she qualified for government sponsored retraining, and upon further checking, the retraining included not only paying for school, but a monthly allowance while in school. The monthly allowance exactly matched her pay at the office!

Today she is an RN and loves what she does and is completely fulfilled. Isn't nursing a gift? Isn't that a God-given gift? (Aren't they all God given?)

Office of nurse?

Now…would we refer to her as 'the office of nurse'? Would we refer to that craftsman as 'the office of woodworker'? Do we refer to DaVinci as the man who stood in the office of artist and the office of scientist? Has anyone ever heard of Isaac Stern as the one who fills the 'office of violinist'?

The same thinking that esteems gifts in these people and segments of society is the way God really intended us to be esteemed. When Dorcas died in Acts 9, the women showed Peter what beautiful coats and other garments she had made—she was esteemed for her gift, but she didn't stand in the 'office of seamstress'.

Remember that God put the functions of the 5-fold at the bottom of his building and to elevate them to 'office' status is to put them at the top of the pyramid. Even though **scripture calls the '5-fold' gifts** (Gk: 'doma') we often hear them called 'office of apostle' and 'office of prophet'. This is due in part because Paul said in Romans 11:13:

"I am the apostle of the Gentiles, I magnify my <u>office.</u>" (KJV)

The word Paul wrote that is translated office is the word 'diakonia', or service.

The modern word 'deacon' comes from this word. Paul is not saying he magnifies himself as an apostle, he is saying he magnifies his service to the Gentiles. Vine brings out that the word 'magnify' (Gk: doxazo) means to magnify or extol. In other words, Paul is literally saying:

"I am the sent one to the Gentiles; I honor and extol my service (to them)."

He is not magnifying some office of apostle, he is magnifying his service to the people he was sent. He is magnifying his function. This understanding is in perfect agreement with Jesus' statement that leadership is at the bottom, and in Paul's own practice of traveling from house to house making disciples and planting churches, staying with the people he ministered to much of the time as he shared Jesus with them.

Another use of the word 'office' is in Romans 12:4, where after listing what are commonly called the 'motivational gifts', Paul observes:

"For as in one physical body we have many parts (organs, members) and all of these parts do not have the same office (function or use)" (AMP)

The word 'office' in the KJV is the Greek word "praxis"—use or function, literally: "a doing, deed" (Vine).

Paul is merely stating the obvious, that though we are all members of the body of Christ, we don't all do the same thing. We don't all have the same function. This context is reinforced by his use of the human body as an example of something that has many parts with each part having a different function, purpose and use. He used the same example again in I Corinthians 12, where he compares the eye to the hand and so forth. Paul did not make a distinction in parts of the body, calling one the "office" of the eye and another "just a part" of the body, making some sort of distinction between the two making one superior to the other. No! His example was that all body parts are equal, just with different functions, or gifts, or abilities.

The word office is used again in I Timothy 3:10, 13.

"...let them use the office of a deacon" and

"...that have used the office of a deacon." (KJV)

Both these words translated 'office' are the same word 'servant' that Paul used to describe his function in Romans 11:13. Paul is acknowledging the servanthood of being a deacon, that word deacon again being 'one who serves'. Therefore in both examples Paul is literally saying:

"...those who serve as servants".

The last place the word 'office' is used in reference to New Testament functions is found in I Timothy 3:1

"If any man desires the office of a bishop..." (I Tim 3:1—KJV)

The word 'office' in this setting is the word 'episkope', or overseer, and the word 'bishop' is essentially the same word. Paul is saying,

"If anyone wants to oversee as an overseer."

There is no 'office' of bishop, deacon or any other gifts, they are just functions...overseeing, serving, and so forth. These are action words, not titles.

Elders in house church?

As I studied the difference between thinking of elders and bishops as offices in the structure of the pyramid traditional church versus the Word putting them forth as functions in the midst of house based churches, I looked for further confirmation in the way they functioned in the house churches of the book of Acts.

In Acts 20:17 Paul calls for the leaders of the house churches in Ephesus to meet him about five miles down the road in Miletus because it is no longer safe for him to go into the city.

He called the 'elders' to him. The word translated 'elder' is the Greek word, presbuteros, an adjective meaning 'an old man'. Literally, Paul called the old men to a meeting. That sort of changes our understanding a bit doesn't it? So we must ask if these gifts really are functions rather than offices like we think of them, then there should be further proof of their function in this passage.

Indeed, verse 28 says:

"Take care and be on guard for yourselves and the whole flock over which the Holy Spirit has appointed you <u>bishops</u> and guardians, to shepherd (<u>pastor</u>) (tend and feed and guide) the church of the Lord which He obtained for Himself (buying it and saving it for Himself) with His own blood." (AMP)

Here in one setting we have the old men (elders) called to a meeting and are told to oversee the flock by tending to them as those called forth conduct the business of the kingdom.

Notice that all three functions—elder, bishop, pastor—are all rolled into one, without any identification of one man being an elder, another a bishop, and yet another the pastor. The whole group serves as 'old men', overseers, and tenders of the sheep.

In I Peter 5:1–2 we see the same thing:

"The <u>elders</u> (old men) that are among you I exhort, who am also an elder...<u>feed (pastor)</u> (shepherd—tend the flock) of God which is

among you, taking the <u>oversight (bishop)</u>...and when the Chief Shepherd shall appear..." (KJV)

Just like Paul, Peter rolls the functions of elder, pastor, and overseer into the same functions. Not titles, he is addressing functions, describing their gift of service. Peter the apostle also calls himself an elder in this passage.

In a home church setting, as in the New Testament, elders are pastors who 'take heed to themselves' meaning they watch over their own walk with God. This brings into their lives the constant reminder of accountability to the Lord. They also seek the well being of the sheep as a first priority. They are people of character and maturity, with adequate life experience and stability to guide others. Their leadership is offered to others, not demanded. They know when to be quiet and let the Lord use others, and when to speak. They are apt to teach, imparting to others what they have learned, though they are usually not gifted in or fill the role of teacher, but rather as father in the faith.

The pyramid shaped traditional church separates the elders from the pastors and the pastors from the bishops in various ways; their roles causing whole denominations to be formed around this issue, but it was not so among the house churches of scripture. The Presbyterians are ruled by elders, the Episcopalians and Catholics by bishops, and most Charismatic and Evangelical churches are governed by pastors, and on it goes.

In scriptural context we can see it is all about function and nothing about title! The titles we assign today in the 21st century merely described functions in the first century. Notice that this council of 'old men' had the joint responsibility of tending the flock. There was no 'pastor' elevated above all. In a house church setting, with gifts esteemed according to where they fit in God's usage, and therefore degree of service rendered, there is mutual accountability among those who are most mature.

The 'pastors' rise from within quite naturally and there may be several within any one house based church. These are the ones to call someone they haven't seen in a while, they are the ones who naturally spend hours on the phone walking a person through a crisis. In the first century the pastors were just such people; they did not have 1 man elevated above all and called 'pastor'. There were many who functioned as those who naturally fed and cared for the sheep. Not an office, but a grace in the heart and gift to the body.

However I can't blame those in the pyramid structure for their various applications of elder, bishops and pastors. After all, when you are forced to interpret the Biblical structure of the New Testament house church through the eyes of the pyramid, there is no easy fit, yet something has to be done with these gifts because they are woven throughout the New Testament, thus the various forms of church government mentioned above.

The word elder is used in the New Testament to emphasize one or all of the following qualities: age, maturity in Christ, and/or maturity in life experience. But the real distinguishing factor is that they 'take heed to themselves' in their faith and lives, and secondarily have a natural love for the sheep.

By contrast, in many traditional churches today the elders may be notable business people, the pastor's relatives, an influential person, a department head, a politically motivated person, or yes man, filling elected or appointed offices depending on denomination or structure.

Paul addresses the character of a person that the function of an overseer/old man/shepherd should have in I Timothy 3: 1–7 and it should be noted that the issue is <u>character and motive</u>.

Many of us have the idea of a bishop or elder or pastor being 'over us' so ingrained because all we've known is the pyramid, that it still presents an image in our minds that seems to contradict Jesus' statements and Paul's teachings about apostles and the '5-fold' being at the bottom of the structure. How can someone who oversees do so from the bottom of a structure?

As Jesus sits in authority as the Head of the Body and Leader of the church at the Father's right hand in heaven, how can he also be the Cornerstone of the foundation, at the bottom of it all looking up at the rest of the building?

<u>Our minds automatically tend to think</u> of these two elements as illustrated on the next page:

As illustrated, apostles, prophets and the 5-fold are at or near the top in terms of authority given by God, but at or near the bottom offering the greatest service, humility, and servant's hearts of any of the gifts.

But the reality is that **great authority is exercised through the burden of great servanthood and responsibility.** As Jesus is entrusted with the greatest authority of all so is he entrusted with the greatest burden of all, overseeing the lives of those he died for.

Hebrews 9:16–17 tells us:

"For where there is a (last) will and testament involved, the death of the one who made it must be established, for a will and testament is valid and takes effect only at death, since it has no force or legal power as long as the one who made it is alive." (AMP)

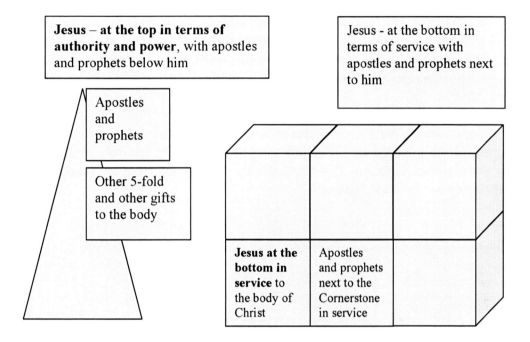

Jesus died to put his will into effect, and then the Father resurrected him so that he could oversee the proper execution of his will. In effect, Jesus was resurrected to become the executor of his own estate. The degree of entrusted authority in a person is proportional to the level of servanthood and responsibility. Jesus died for all so he was given the burden and responsibility to oversee all.

The apostle Paul noted in II Corinthians 11:22–33 everything that he had suffered in terms of physical hardship and persecution for the sake of the gospel, and then added in verse 28:

"Beside those things that are on the outside, that which comes upon me daily, the care of all the churches." (KJV)

Paul also said he was assigned an 'angel of Satan' to buffet him lest he be exalted above measure because of the greatness of the revelations he'd received. When he asked the Lord to remove this demonic assignment, he told him 'My grace is sufficient for you." In other words, Paul had to learn to deal with the onslaughts and walk out his own salvation.

"For it seems to me that God has made an exhibit of us apostles, exposing us to view last (of all, like men in a triumphal procession who are) sentenced to death (and displayed at the end of the line). For we have become a spectacle to the world (a show in the world's amphitheater) with both men and angels (as spectators). (I Cor 4:9 AMP)

Therefore the reality and secret of Jesus' church structure is not Jesus sitting at the top of the pyramid as our minds tend to think in the illustration above, but rather the lines of authority flow through the burden of great servanthood and responsibility as illustrated below.

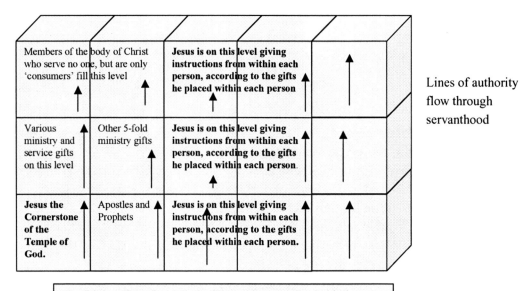

Members of the body of Christ who serve no one, but are only 'consumers' fill this level

Jesus is on this level giving instructions from within each person, according to the gifts he placed within each person

Various ministry and service gifts on this level

Other 5-fold ministry gifts

Jesus is on this level giving instructions from within each person, according to the gifts he placed within each person.

Jesus the Cornerstone of the Temple of God.

Apostles and Prophets

Jesus is on this level giving instructions from within each person, according to the gifts he placed within each person.

Lines of authority flow through servanthood

The Living Temple of God – Through mutual submission bound by love and honoring each other's gifts, the whole body is built up. Those in greatest authority have proportional responsibility and servanthood required.

This is the Great Balance of the Father's design with Jesus as the greatest example. Jesus was the most gifted and the greatest servant rolled into one. Therefore he is the most highly exalted Man in the universe, seated at the Father's own right hand. By giving men great authority and power, often with signs and wonders happening in their ministries, the Father tempered any tendency for pride by making those same people the greatest servants of all.

This is perfectly logical from the Father's perspective: **By giving the 5-fold the greatest authority while at the same time burdening them with the greatest servanthood, He assures they will be humble, transparent, and approachable—pride should not be an issue for anyone so gifted and yet so burdened.** (If they function in the structure Jesus portrayed).

This is why Acts 2:42 and 46 tells us the apostles were among the people as they: "devoted themselves constantly to the instruction and fellowship of the apostles, to the breaking of bread and prayers" and "from house to house". Paul also said of his time in Ephesus that he spoke publicly and from house to house (Acts 20:20). Paul and Peter are seen staying with people in their homes throughout the book of Acts (as opposed to an Inn).

The apostles were not away from the people at the top of some pyramid isolated in an office and only dealing with their top assistants, they lived among and spent time with the people, just as Jesus had.

Apostles spend time with the people they serve because they want to, because the making of disciples burns within them. Therefore **one of the benchmarks of an apostle is the time spent with those they serve.**

There is a balance however: In Acts 13:1 the text names certain "prophets and teachers" meeting together to pray, and when Paul and Barnabus came to Jerusalem in the council of Acts 15 it says the "elders and apostles" came together to consider the matter", not the whole of the church.

Therefore it is obvious that apostles will spend time with other leaders, but apostles will also spend much of their time with the people they serve.

What about an office staff?

This does not mean a modern apostle can't have an office staff with lines of authority flowing to the staff, but the flow is upward and through them to others, empowering them as well as giving direction for the ministry. In fact, if you look at how Jesus governed his 12 disciples we can get a glimpse of the house church model. The model is that of very limited control, choosing rather to perceive a person's gift, put them in charge of something where their gift will flow, and then oversee as a spiritual parent from a distance, coming alongside when needed, rather than that of a top down flow structure of the corporate world.

For instance Jesus sent the 12 and then later 70 out to minister as they had seen him, and their only mechanism of oversight was to give him a report when they came back, in the case of the 70 rejoicing that even the demons were subject to his name.

On the Mount of Transfiguration Jesus took with him Peter, James and John, leaving the other 9 to minister without them. When he came down from the mountain Mark 9:14 says this:

"And when he came to his disciples he saw a great multitude about them, and the scribes questioning with them." (KJV)

It was in this setting that the man who had the son with seizures came to him stating that his disciples could not cast out the spirit. The point is that Jesus tried to duplicate himself by perceiving a person's gifts and letting them flow. In this example the setting is spiritual giftings. Also remember that in John 6:5 Jesus saw a multitude of people and asked the disciples how they were going to feed them all, as the text says:

"and this he said to test him (Philip), for he himself knew what he would do." (KJV)

In Acts 6 the question about what to do in the feeding program came up and the apostles replied to the multitude of disciples in verses 3–4:

"Therefore select out from among yourselves, brethren, seven men of good and attested character and repute, full of the Holy Spirit and wisdom, whom we may assign to look after this business and duty. But we will continue to devote ourselves steadfastly to prayer and the ministry of the Word." (AMP)

The apostles really didn't want to run a food program, but notice the people selected those gifted for just such a task. While the pyramid promotes micro-management, the Building of God allows for empowerment and freedom to act independently.

If Jesus had been at the top of a pyramid he would never have empowered the 12 and then the 70 to minister. He would never have asked Phillip how they were going to feed all those people. If the apostles ran a pyramid they would have given direct orders about how they wanted the food program run and then watched over it very carefully lest something be done differently than how they would have done it.

One house church has a ministry to Mexican children in a predominantly Mexican trailer park. The leaders are very good about empowering those interested in helping no matter their church affiliation and plugging them in to the area of ministry that fits their giftings. If they were at the top of a pyramid they would assign people based solely on the needs at that moment and carefully watch to make sure all is being done as they would do.

The focus of the apostles in Acts 6 was that they could continue to minister, which the text says they went from house to house and the people were in the apostles fellowship and doctrine. (Acts 2:42, 46). When they said they wanted to continue to give themselves to prayer, study, and the ministry of the Word they meant they wanted to remain free to be among the people they served.

Most of those who call themselves 'apostles' today actually sit atop a pyramid and do not spend most of their time ministering to small groups in homes, but rather in large meetings and they deal with leaders almost exclusively. In the flat structure Jesus advocated there is a constant flow and mix of leaders and those new to the Lord. The primary role of apostles is church planting in homes, and furthering the discipleship process in people.

It is sad to say that when I have gone to many homes and small group meetings some people express surprise I am willing to do so. To me, this is what being an apostle is all about, sharing the revelation and wisdom I have with those hungry for more.

I have seen the occasional minister try to balance the two. One traveling teacher with a healing gifting as well that I know goes two weeks of every month to larger venues where the offerings and product sales are larger, then two weeks to small groups. He depends on the larger venues to pay for his trips to the smaller venues, and this is admirable I think, as I know the struggles of finances when ministering to small groups compared to larger ones.

So we see the check and balance in God's Kingdom—the greater the authority, the greater servanthood and responsibility required as Jesus had taught in Mark 10:42–46—which keeps a person balanced out. Combined with walking in love and mutual accountability, the body of Christ and leaders in particular, are naturally approachable, available, humble and transparent.

By contrast, the pyramid often has no check and balance, for the person at the top is accountable to no one, and also the one in whom all authority resides. (With pride and arrogance often becoming increasingly apparent over time) If there is a system of checks and balances, it's often in the form of a board or trustees who are 'yes men' to the leader.

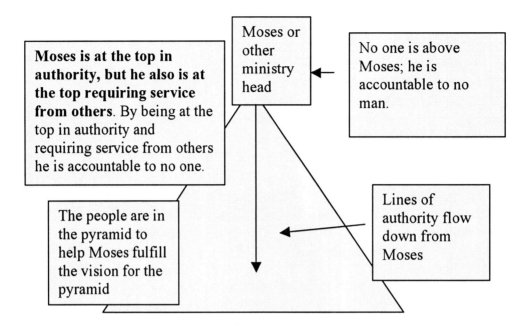

Jesus Himself is the greatest example of Ultimate authority coupled with Ultimate humility, love, and servanthood with the 5-fold placed right next to him at the bottom of the living temple, the people of God. My observation has been that most of the true apostles and 5-fold within the structure Jesus and the New Testament teaches, those truly burdened with a heart to serve because they know what they've been given, are the multitudes out there busy building God's kingdom, not their own, largely unknown by the general populace.

From the Old Testament references of the Messiah being the Cornerstone to Paul's references about the Body of Christ becoming a holy habitation built upon the Cornerstone, to Peter's illustration of we believers being living stones, we come to understand the building we are talking about is a <u>living building</u>.

Jesus, the firstborn from the dead and Cornerstone of the foundation oversees the rest of this organism of a building in service from the bottom up, adjusting where needed, adding on here, sanding rough edges or rearranging over there.

There is an additional dimension that Jesus adds to the living temple by virtue of being exalted at the right hand of the Father. He has the capacity to be everywhere and in everyone within the building. Unlike a flow chart illustrating lines of authority from one man to another dictated from above, Jesus lives within each person in the body of Christ.

Though exalted above all, he remains the servant of all, from within all. Everything around us in the world is a pyramid—our work, the traditional church—so how do we understand the church as Jesus and Paul presented it?

The only way to have someone in authority overseeing the Body from the bottom up is to <u>utilize natural gifts and functions controlled by love rather than job description</u>. Consider that the ministry of Jesus has not ended. He has never stopped serving! In the same way he exhibited all authority over the wind and waves yet washed the disciple's feet, he is still serving mankind today!

Chapter 7

God Living Among and Through His People

Ephesians 4:8 says Jesus gave gifts to men. But Ephesians 4: 8 is a quote from Psalm 68:18. Paul only quoted the first part of this verse and his point was made, however by looking at the rest of this verse we can see the fullness of the Lord's thought.

Psalm 68:18 says:

"You have ascended up on high, you have led captivity captive: you have received gifts for men (quoted in Ephesians 4:8); <u>yea, for the rebellious also, that the Lord God might dwell among them.</u>" (KJV)

"For the rebellious also <u>that the Lord God might live among them</u>" Wow! The gifts were given so that God could live among the rebellious, not to be locked away in some building and seen only on a Sunday morning. He wants to live among the rebellious, and he does this by people flowing in their gifts! Remember the Genesis command to fill the earth, and how God is seeking to fill the earth. He wants to live among the people and this is evidenced by his choosing to live in us instead of apart from us in a building.

Suddenly another element of my 'religious' thinking revealed itself. For years I had subconsciously thought the gifts were mainly for Sunday morning in the auditorium style service, and would be harder to 'flow' on the street. But I remembered that Jesus did most of his miracles outside the synagogue. Water into wine at a wedding, deaf ears opened along the road, blind men approaching him at dinner, a man raised from the dead at his own funeral, a little girl raised from the dead in her bedroom, and on it goes.

In fact, most of Jesus' miracles were interruptions as he was just going about his business! <u>Most of Jesus' miracles were interruptions to his schedule</u>.

I started to realize that a house church setting was the most natural place in the world for the Lord to perform miracles and answer prayers, for it affords the most spontaneity and flexibility for the Lord to be able to meet the needs as he sees fit. The home remains the most natural place for a person to grow into their gifts.

I had relegated miracles to Sunday morning service, thinking, "If I could just get so and so to a service so they could see…" This was further evidence of my pyramid mentality rather than a scripturally minded concept of church.

The Marketplace

The revelation that the gifts Jesus gave to men are so that he might live among the 'unsaved' is completely opposite the way most of us were trained in the faith, but completely consistent with house church and what I call "Relationship Based Christianity". We have been trained to try to bring people to a church building instead of taking the church building to the people in the form of YOU, you are the church building, and you live right there among them.

We haven't understood the words of Jesus in Mt 11:19 as understood within their context in the first century:

> **"The Son of Man came eating and drinking (with others), and they say, Behold, a glutton and a wine drinker, a friend of tax collectors and (especially wicked) sinners! Yet wisdom is justified and vindicated by what she does (her deeds) and by her children." (AMP)**

We have understood this verse through the pyramid's eyes, admiring Jesus from a distance living among the people (he could do that because he is Lord), but now relegating that ministry to those who are called to 'those kinds of people', the rougher segment of society.

We have not understood that Jesus was living and traveling and talking among these people, living life with them, visiting their homes and businesses, teaching about the kingdom of God to all who would listen.

Such is the nature of house based church. Instead of calling people out of their neighborhoods, 'Hey, come to our church this Sunday', house church takes God to the neighborhoods and to their living rooms. Jesus hangs out in the neighborhoods if he lives in you and you are being the church.

Then they may say of you, 'He hangs out with those sinners in the neighborhood, attending their BBQs where they serve beer and people smoke, he is a friend of sinners'. Then you can be counted with Jesus, and in that day rejoice! As St. Francis of Assisi is quoted; "Witness for the Lord at all times, and when necessary, use words." <u>Much of what Jesus accomplished was so because he was there when events unfolded around him.</u>

He was at a wedding minding his own business when they ran out of wine. He was on his way to Jairus' house when the woman with the hemorrhaging touched him, he was on his way out of Jericho when Bartimaeus called to him. We must be where life happens because the gifts were given so God could live among the rebellious!

Marketplace ministries

All we've known was that the pastor was the one called into the ministry. Those in business and the marketplace were made to feel like second class citizens. **Those in business were looked upon as citizens of the kingdom with a lesser call on their lives**, subject to the church and pastor. For all anyone knew, the pastor was the only one called and gifted by God.

This mindset has set up a massive conflict within the business person. Their businesses and employees are the source of funds for the church, but they are often made to feel inferior or not as called. Also, in a pyramid structure the pastor oversees an archaic administrative structure that often spends money unwisely and is highly inefficient while the business person is used to scrutinizing every dollar and changing and adapting to meet the needs of the customer.

The church has had the same structure since the dark ages (literally) and the business person cringes at the thought of giving money into such an inefficiently run organization.

I was part of a meeting that included business people within a church who were invited for their input to a proposed program. One business owner, upon entering the room said tongue in cheek: "Are you calling us here to tell us we aren't giving enough, or do you have some project you want us to fund?"

This way of thinking is a product of the Jethro pyramid. It's an 'us versus them' mentality. What bothers the pastor in this structure is that the business person operates outside the pyramid and they know how to think for themselves, so they can't be controlled, unlike most sheep in the pew, who follow along without examining what is told them. The pastor needs their money but the business people have trouble giving to such an inefficient organization, especially if their call to business is not recognized from the pulpit. When the Lord was teaching me these things he said:

> **"Remember that I am the giver of all gifts. The gift of apostle to the church is what the world calls entrepreneur. Men put different labels on the gifts, but remember that the gifts come from me."**

I asked for a confirmation in scripture and he told me, "Look at the life of Paul in Corinth." When I examined the life of Paul in Acts 18: 1–3, I saw that by trade Paul was a tent maker. I knew from study that Corinth held the 'Isthmian games' every two years, a smaller version of the Olympics, and that tents and awnings were in demand much like we see today at fairs and festivals. Tent makers in this culture dealt with wool, dyes for the wool, leather, wood, marketing, and sales.

I understood that Paul was an entrepreneur. The same gifts that enabled Paul to enter a strange city and set up his business, dealing with the assembly of parts, manufacture, marketing and sales, were the same gifts that enabled him to go into a strange city and start a church, flowing as apostle, teacher, pastor, and church leader.

Suddenly I realized something in my own life. All my life I have been used of the Lord in the business realm to start businesses, or to restructure and rebuild them. In the ministry I have been used to restructure, start, or rebuild churches and church related programs. It is the same gift of apostle, but that gift can flow through most any structure.

I suddenly saw that God truly gifted each person with talents, motivations, and personalities that have their source in God's own personality.

There is no difference between the sacred and the secular

The thinking that the 'clergy is called of God but I'm not' is part of the Jethro pyramid way of thinking which makes a separation between the sacred and the secular. We have been trained to think we are either inside the pyramid or outside the pyramid. Inside is sacred and outside is secular. "Church is sacred, but I work a secular job." The New Testament, realizing Christ lives in us and we are therefore temples of God, says in Romans 1:17:

> **'...the just shall live by (his) faith'. (KJV)**

Christ lives in us. Where we are, so is Christ. In him we live and move and have our being. Therefore there is no line between sacred and secular. **For us, all is sacred.**

There have been times I've held a job or owned my own business while continuing work in the ministry, but have felt like I was a second class citizen for having to work a secular job. But now I realized as a temple of God I was taking the Lord with me wherever I went and whatever I did. To the New Testament disciple there is no such thing as 'secular'. Because I am a temple of God whatever I own and use is sacred, separated unto God for God's business.

My mentality had been temple based, that the temple is holy and I had to go there to hear from God, instead of Truth based, wherein I am the temple of God and all that I am and all that I possess in this world is sacred.

Being temples of God we, and everything with which we are involved, is sacred. We are a kingdom of priests and just like the Old Testament priests, all our belongings as well as we ourselves, is sacred.

That means your car is sacred. Your cubicle at work is sacred. Your children are sacred. Your dishwasher is sacred. All are dedicated to the Lord's work because he lives in you, the temple of God. This is why Paul could say in I Corinthians 7:14 that in an unequally yoked marriage, the unbelieving spouse is sanctified (sacred, set apart for God).

In part, this is why the Holy Spirit is grieved when your TV, DVD, computer, radio, and so forth, are used by the devil to impart impure things into you. Paul's admonition to not grieve the Spirit of God in Ephesians 4:30 takes on new meaning when you consider he was speaking to people in their home based churches, as he is to us in house church today. Therefore, your gifts and talents are sacred and wherever they are manifest, so also Christ is manifest.

I taught this one day and a man told me "You saved my life." He went on to explain that he owned a heating and air conditioning business and felt called into the ministry, and that's why he was at Bible school.

But he also believed the Lord told him he was called as an apostle in the marketplace and he had a genuine call of God to his business. He had never received any affirmation of his call from the pulpit, in fact only the opposite was communicated. He had been inwardly tormented by feeling he had to leave his work to go 'into the ministry'. I assured him that by moving in his gift and call to the heating and air conditioning industry, God was living among the rebellious and he was fulfilling his call and purpose in life.

As he was installing and repairing furnaces and air conditioners around town, the Lord God was living among the rebellious. As he and his staff prayerfully sought God's wisdom in how to install the systems, God was living among the rebellious and manifesting His wisdom and ways.

As he was praying about his employee's health care plan and receiving wisdom, God was living among the rebellious. He had heard correctly when the Lord told him he was an apostle in business. I've watched him over the years and he starts and buys up other businesses, spreading his business model wherever he can, in the same way an apostle establishes churches in homes wherever he can.

I began to understand that God was living among the heathen through the gifts he had given to his body all along, and the church world had been missing it for years by confining their thinking to inside the pyramid. For too long I'd talked to men and women who truly loved their jobs and felt called to be in business, but felt they had to leave it and go to Bible school to 'go into the ministry'. I realized how this was wrong thinking for most people. They too didn't realize they were in the ministry already.

Without knowing it, my thinking had been the Jethro pyramid while trying to flow in the New Testament apostolic.

Gifts and Labels

Though man-made labels vary depending on the structure they are functioning in, the gifts are the same God-given gifts; they just flow differently depending on the structure they are placed in. I asked a Bible school class full of adults who were in their second year of ministry training how many were called to be pastors. The classes' thinking was that of the traditional pyramid—they envisioned themselves one day earning a living overseeing a church somewhere.

Of those students who responded I found out that most were earning their living as managers in various levels of business and that they loved those they worked with. Their employees came to them for advice and help of a personal nature over and above work issues. They genuinely loved their coworkers and imparted to them wisdom and caring beyond their mere job definitions.

Until that moment they had not realized they were already manifesting the gift of a pastor. They thought that a person was called as a pastor, which meant that gift only functioned in a traditional style church, the pyramid. So they had to go to a Bible school, graduate, and find a church to pastor for their gift to be activated. They thought the gift only flowed within the four walls of a traditional church.

The realization that a pastor is a gift, literally one who tends the flock or herd, and that ability is something that flows naturally from within those who have it whatever structure it's given, was totally new. They suddenly saw their jobs in a whole new light. They were actually pastoring their coworkers, because the gift of tending the flock manifests in whatever structure it's given.

Pastors shepherd sheep, they care for them, sympathize and empathize with people. These students showed they were operating in the gift of pastor right there at work, even though their title was 'manager' or 'director', or something similar. Man gives the job titles, but God give the gifts. Adam was given the authority to name things, and man has been doing it ever since, but the gifts come from God.

In many classes and churches I have asked for a show of hands of those called to evangelism. This includes those called to missions, short term mission trips, outreaches of various kinds, and in general, winning people to Christ. Of those who raised their hands, I asked what kinds of jobs they had. Nearly every one has answered sales, marketing, or recruiting. It's the same gift of evangelist, but different title.

As funny as it sounds, the gift that explains to a person why they need Jesus, is the same gift that gives them insight into why that customer needs that new car. Some people are born salespeople and born to win strangers to Christ, and others are gifted to minister to the body of Christ, though as already illustrated, we should all be ready to share Christ with those in our own spheres of influence.

Next I asked for those called to be teachers. A few hands went up and I asked what they did for a living. Most were in job training, career counseling, teaching, and some in marketing. Some were lawyers or trainers in some fashion. They just naturally taught people different aspects of their discipline. It is the same gift, but receives different titles in the world.

I asked about those who felt a prophetic call. The answers to what they did for a living included accounting, human resources, law, jobs involving making policy, jobs involving ethics and legal issues. As I taught they came to realize that the same gift that allowed that accountant to tell the CEO where his company would be in 1 year was the same insightful gift God uses as the prophetic. The gift that enabled the HR person to look down the road to see where the company needed to make changes, also enabled them to receive words of knowledge and wisdom for people during prayer concerning decisions that needed to be made in that person's life.

We have a pyramid mentality if we limit our understanding of gifts to the 5 mentioned in Ephesians 4:11 and the charismatic gifts of I Corinthians 12 or even the 'motivational gifts' of Romans 12:6–8. There are many more mentioned in the Bible, and I suppose there are many more not mentioned. Actually, the first gifts mentioned in the Bible are found in Genesis 4:21 concerning Jabal, the father of those who "play the lyre and pipe".

The next specific passages related to God's giftings concern craftsmen and women who built the tabernacle and these scriptures give us insight to understanding the basis for how the gifts operate, even in the house based church.

"...And I have filled him with the spirit of God, in wisdom, and in understanding, and in knowledge, and in all manner of workmanship...and in the hearts of all that are wisehearted I have put wisdom, that they may make all that I have commanded." (Ex 31:3, 6—KJV)

"...and every wisehearted among you shall come and make all that the Lord has commanded...and they came, every one whose heart stirred him up...and all the women whose heart stirred them up in wisdom spun goats hair...every man and woman whose heart made them willing to bring all manner of work which the Lord had commanded to be made..." (Ex 35:10, 21, 26, 29—KJV)

Gifts are something given by God when the person was created. People are born with an ability that is unique to their personality, and they are most fulfilled (therefore) when flowing in these gifts. They aren't activated when a person is born again (enhanced and developed—yes of course), for God is the creator of the human spirit and he has created each person with the ability to flow with Him in their giftings—whether they choose to follow God or not.

Like the craftsmen and women mentioned in Exodus above, our gifts stir us from within, and we have an internal knowledge of how to do that particular thing.

This is why house church is the highest and best 'structure' for church. With each person empowered and flowing in their gifts, and others perceiving those gifts, we extend the hand of fellowship (Gal 2:9) and learn to appreciate each other. Whether it was the women who valued the coats and clothes Dorcas had made (Acts 9:39) or appreciation for Luke being a doctor or Zenas the lawyer, or even the women of Herod's staff supporting Jesus in ministry (Lk 8:3), we are to flow in our gifts as God designed us, for we are all sacred, all we touch is sacred, and we see elements of God's personality in each other in this way.

In a Bible class, when I ask for those called to helps in the church, I find they volunteer in areas of clerical or other support, even the nursery and bus ministry, and in their jobs they are often administrative assistants, clerks, secretaries, lower level management and customer service, in other words 'front line' people. They do the same type of work in the ministry of helps on Sunday as they do at their job Monday through Friday; it's the same gift flowing within different structures.

When I ask about 'governments', I find people who earn a living in law, insurance, accounting and the like, while volunteering to help the church with it's by-laws, accounting, areas a trustee would oversee, and so on.

Jesus is the greatest gift, with all other gifts flowing from him, so they will all flow in his spirit of humility and service. The gifts are to be seen among the unsaved, and only a few of those gifts are the charismatic gifts or 'ministry' gifts, which is the normal way we view this concept. Jesus took the gift to the people rather than hiding it away.

So it is today. He's never changed. He is still going into homes and work places manifesting Himself through his people, we've just misunderstood and at times, worked against him in His efforts.

The Gifts are the Personality of God

I started hearing testimonies from the people I was teaching that went something like this: "I was trying to help this lady finance a new car that she really needed but we were at a dead end, then suddenly the Lord showed me to call one person in particular in the finance department, and he put it through for her." (Car salesman, called to be an evangelist)

Or:"I was at my desk going through some paperwork and suddenly this guy who works in our department came to mind with a real burden to pray for him. I went down the hall and talked to him and he just found out his wife's condition had taken a turn for the worse and was very upset." (Man called to be a pastor)

I heard one fiery preacher say that the Lord speaks to him very sternly and matter of fact, and realized that was because the preacher is stern and matter of fact.

I saw that when a person had a laid back personality God would deal with them over the course of months or even years, and someone who was more cut and dried related that God really dealt with them about right and wrong and they had to get their act together right then. I noticed musicians largely only heard from God when they were playing their instrument and teachers heard from God primarily through the Word.

I noticed people who loved nature heard from the Lord most clearly while out of doors, and people gifted in finance seemed to have the Lord speak to them of His plans for them and others in very organized and clearly defined ways. I came to realize that

God relates to you according to the gifts he placed in you.

Because He placed that element of His personality in you that relates to music, he will speak to you directly through music, showing you what he thinks in a given situation as it relates to that gift.

Because he placed that element of His personality in you that relates to the precision of numbers, he will speak to you from that element of his personality, expressing to you ideas from that perspective.

We all have many different aspects of His personality, but a few will rise to the top to become the predominant one(s), and these aspects of his personality will become the context of how he will speak to us.

Consider Joseph in Genesis 37. We are shown in the text that Joseph has a gift for administration, and is his father's foreman. Twice he is seen being told by his father to go and check on his brothers and the flocks and to report back (v2, 14).

Because Joseph clearly has the gift of administration, the dreams God gives him reflect a sense of order and purpose. One dream is sheaves in the field, already tied up neatly and in a row, all bowing down to him. Another dream is that of the sun, moon and stars bowing down to him, and even in ancient times the orderliness and precision of the universe were known and appreciated. God spoke to Joseph in terms that his gifts would understand.

The dreams Joseph would later interpret that the dreamers themselves did not understand, were all orderly and administrative in nature. Chapter 40 tells of a dream with a vine and three branches, blossoms and Pharaoh's cup. The Baker's dream consisted of three white baskets with baked goods in the top basket, but birds came and ate them. Pharaoh's own dream was equally orderly: Seven starving cows eating seven fat cows; and seven fat ears of grain being devoured by seven thin heads of grain.

Each dream was orderly, precise, and perfectly suited for Joseph's gift of administration. God will speak to you according to your gifts.

Romans 1 says the physical world illustrates the spiritual, so if we look at the attributes of light we can understand this clearer. Visible white light is made up of several colors, which we see in a rainbow when raindrops act as a prism to split the light into its colors: Red, orange, yellow, green, blue, indigo and violet. These all are within visible light.

God is light, and he like a prism has split himself into different aspects of his personality and placed those elements in each of us. In the same way those 7 colors are always in light but only seen when the light runs through the prism, God Himself is in all our personalities, but we only see the completeness of him as we see ALL the gifts in ourselves and each other, coming into the unity of the body of Christ.

The element of God's personality the fiery preacher has in which God speaks to him bluntly is one element of God's personality and just as valid as the laid back man who says God speaks to him very gently and over the course of time. Both are parts of those 'colors' of Light.

A friend commented that her four daughters have giftings that naturally clash and have caused friction in the past. But she observed and then told them one day that because she was their mother and part of her was in each one of them, she could relate to each one accordingly and there was no conflict with her. That is how it is with our heavenly Father…he gave part of himself to create each of us and therefore he relates with, and relates to, that part in us. It's up to us to love that part of him in each other.

This is why the flat structure of house church is the most efficient at allowing the different aspects of God's personality to come forth in a meeting; whereas in the pyramid the only aspects of God's personality they see week after week is the preacher and maybe some musicians. The pyramid is one dimensional, house church is multi-dimensional. A service in a pyramid styled church is designed to keep people from participating (except for the designated few) while house church is geared that all may take part.

Everyone therefore has combinations of gifts within them. In I Corinthians 12:4–7 Paul lists 3 main categories of gifts but says they all come from the same Spirit:

> **"Now there are diversities of gifts (Gk: charisma—charismatic gifts)**
>
> **…and there are differences in administrations (Gk: diakonia—service)**
>
> **…and there are diversities of operations (Gk: energei—energies/motivations)**
>
> **…but the <u>manifestation of the Spirit is given to everyone to profit.</u>" (KJV)**

Notice he says that these are all manifestations of the Spirit of God. We must remove the thinking that only the charismatic gifts are evidence of God moving. The fact that he says service gifts which include the 5-fold; and energy gifts, or motivational gifts are the manifestation of the Spirit cannot be ignored.

That means when a person is serving by setting up chairs because that is their gift—to serve others behind the scenes—it is a manifestation of the Holy Spirit at work as assuredly as someone prophesying or giving a tongue and interpretation.

This means that when someone like Dorcas was serving by making coats and other items of clothing, moving in her gifts, it was a manifestation of the Holy Spirit given that all may profit.

It means when someone who loves the people calls someone who has been on their heart to inquire how they are doing, it is a manifestation of the Spirit given that they may profit.

When you are moving in whom you are, the gifts that make you unique, it is the manifestation of the Spirit of God.

The motivational or 'energy' gifts of Romans 12 provide good examples that these are manifestations of the Spirit.

Paul says in Romans 12:3–6 in part:

"For I say <u>through the grace given to me</u>...God has given to everyone the measure of faith, for as we have different body parts, all the parts don't have the same function. So we being many are one body in Christ; and every one members of each other. Having then gifts that differ according to the grace given to us..." (NKJV)

Notice that Paul said he was speaking through the grace given to him. He could not speak through the grace given to Peter, to speak exclusively to the Jews, for that was Peter's grace. Paul could only speak through his grace.

I remember when I was a Campus Minister on the University of Colorado in Boulder, Colorado. We held services and Bible studies, Christian concerts and guest speakers, all of which came very natural for me to do. But I thought every campus minister ought to be able to preach an evangelistic message, something that wasn't natural for me.

I set up a loud speaker and microphone in the commons area one day, flipped the power on, and was all set to preach a great evangelistic message, but I couldn't think of a single reason why anyone should get saved! My mind went blank. I stumbled over a few words, got a few brief looks but was largely ignored, and shut it down inside of 3 minutes.

Evangelism is not my gift. I don't have the grace for it, and therefore God would not flow through me in that way. I am called to the body of Christ to teach and minister and that is the grace I have, thus God flows through that grace.

He can't flow through a grace he hasn't given you, and that is why Paul said 'through the grace given to me.'

In this passage Paul goes on to mention the energy gift of <u>prophecy</u>, not the charismatic gift or even preaching, but the 'energy' or 'motivation' which is how these people see life. People with a prophecy gifting see things like a prophet: Cut and dried, right or wrong. They are blunt, usually tact is a learned skill, and they have a desire for righteousness in themselves and others, and are loners to a degree. (Elijah and John the Baptist are 2 examples, though they were also prophets)

Other gifts include <u>teachers</u>. They like to tell everyone something they learned or how to do things right; <u>exhorters</u> who like to tell stories about their experiences, believing others will be lifted up if they tell their story; <u>servers</u>, who have a hard time saying 'no' to any need required, they like to be in the background and meet physical needs of people; <u>'ruling'</u> or administration, these people know how to organize anything, but sometimes put the task ahead of the people; <u>giving</u>, these people love to give quietly and love to see their giving make a difference but have to guard against manipulating others by their giving; <u>mercy</u>, these folks identify with the emotions of others, tend to be emotional, but love to provide hospitality and support to people.

Even a brief look at these seven gifts will show us that these graces come from God, and we have them as a reflection of his own personality. Consider that within Jesus we see the prophecy motive as he looks at Peter and tells him, 'Get behind me Satan'. But we also see mercy when he tells the woman caught in adultery, 'Neither do I condemn thee, go and sin no more.'

Teaching and exhorting gifts can be seen by the way Jesus taught and told parables, and no one could argue that he became the servant of all in his life, death, and resurrection.

We also see Jesus with organizing and administrative gifts by the way he made the people sit down in groups of 50s and 100s as he fed the 5,000, and he must have been quite a giver, for when Judas leaves after dinner to betray him around 9pm, the disciples assumed he was leaving to give money to the poor. (John 13:29)

So we, being individual parts of a Great Body, have different gifts which are naturally in us. When we flow in them, we are letting a part of the personality of God flow through us, thus allowing him to live among the rebellious.

The reason the pyramid structure is so stifling is that it allows only a handful of gifts to function at any given time.

Contrary to Paul's observation that 'every one of you may have a psalm, teaching, revelation, gift of the Spirit' in I Corinthians 14:26, the pyramid is designed to limit involvement for the purpose of control.

Sunday after Sunday in a pyramid structured church people in the pews with gifts from God, elements of his personality, are just sitting like bystanders at a parade, watching a few designated people walk in their gifts.

By contrast, house church is a flat structure, designed not to limit participation, but to encourage it, allowing anyone who wishes to share what God is showing or telling them, within the bounds of love and social considerations.

Chapter 8

The Missing Link

All gifts are given by God for his purposes, no matter how we earn a living. How many times have you heard someone say, whether Christian or not, "I quit my job to go do what I really wanted to do" or "I left my position to do what I am really passionate about". And often they will make a statement like, "I was born to do this". They are telling the truth. They are moving in God's giftings to them; multi-faceted and formed deep within, we all have these gifts.

Consider that Paul exhorts the older women to teach the younger, older men the younger. Why? It is because the sharing of our gifts encourages and promotes the development of those gifts in others, and within the Relationship Based Christianity of the house church, multi-generational impartation is a natural occurrence.

This means that the impartation of the gifts and skills within us into the lives of others causes God to flow through us to others.

The Main Purpose of the 5-fold

Therefore <u>the 5-fold ministry gifts job is one of empowering the saints to move into and learn to function in their gifts IN DAILY LIFE, not a church program.</u> Specifically Ephesians 4:12 says

"…for the equipping of the saints for the work of the <u>ministry</u> for the edifying of the body of Christ." (KJV)

The word 'ministry' here again, is the word 'service'. In our pyramid thinking we automatically switch over to think of ministry as something we do. In fact I hesitated writing about this verse because it's almost like the Malachi 3 verse on tithing used to condemn and motivate congregations negatively to such an extent that most of us mentally turn off our minds when it's brought up. Within that context it sounds like pastors are telling their people it's their job to train people for the ministry.

We have to lose that thinking. We must remember that Paul is writing from within a context of house church to people in house church and the flow of multi-generational and close relationships of house churches that develop when you share the same sofa and meals week after week.

The apostles and the 5-fold at the bottom and within a house based and relationship based Christianity wherein people flow with their God given gifts. Within that context the job of the 5-fold is to equip the saints for serving one another.

> **5-fold leadership is marked by the ability to perceive the grace of God in a person's life and help them move into the place of service to others within their sphere of influence, functioning in that grace, rather than in a church structure program. We are gifted to serve each other, not programs.**

Again, Galatians 2:9:

> **"And when they knew (perceived, recognized, understood, and acknowledged) the grace (God's unmerited favor and spiritual blessing) that had been bestowed up me, James and Peter and John, who were reputed to be pillars of the Jerusalem church, gave to me and Barnabas the right hand of fellowship, with the understanding that we should go to the Gentiles and they to the Jews." (AMP)**

Peter, James and John perceived the grace of God in Paul and Barnabas and once perceived, empowered them to go to their ministry to the non-Jewish people groups. The key is perceiving the grace in one another.

At the end of his life Peter would write of Paul's ministry and state flat out that some things Paul says are hard for him to understand:

> **"...even as our beloved brother Paul also wrote to you according to the spiritual insight given him. Speaking of this as he does in all of his letters. There are some thing in those (epistles of Paul) that are difficult to understand, which the ignorant and unstable twist and misconstrue to their own utter destruction, just as (they distort and misinterpret) the rest of the Scriptures." (II Peter 3: 15–16 AMP)**

Peter not only said some things Paul wrote were hard to understand, but he also called his writings scripture, noting that some twist them as they do 'the rest of the Scriptures.'

This indicates that you don't have to understand a person and their life story in order to love them. You can perceive the grace in them, what God has done for them and in them, and love that grace, thus you can enter into a healthy relationship with them.

The purpose of the 5-fold is to enable everyone to flow in their work of service—and that is not on Sunday morning in a traditional pyramid structure, but rather out in life, on the job and in the home.

Paul said in II Cor 5:16:

"...henceforth we know no man after the flesh..." KJV)

Paul's heart was to know people by their spirits, by the grace God has deposited within them. It is to this end that Peter also writes:

"...as everyone has received the gift (grace), even so minister the same one to another, as good stewards of the varied grace of God." (I Peter 4:10—KJV)

The example of Jesus teaching, preaching, and healing while living with his disciples in a sense of community is the pattern for today. The Jethro method is relationships built around work, and then everyone goes home. Jesus' example is relationships walking through life together, perceiving the grace in each other and ministering (serving) the same to each other.

This cannot happen in a pyramid shaped organization because its structure is about empowering the main man and keeping everyone else silent. In the flat structure portrayed by Jesus and the writers of the NT, each person is free to operate as God created them, in their own gifts, while submitting to one another in love.

The pyramid is built that the top man might be in the spotlight and other staff members are just players on the stage. That is 180 degrees from what Jesus said the church should look like. It is a testimony to God's grace that he can flow through it at all, and a key to understanding why the church has become irrelevant to people outside 'the church'. When a structure is built to empower the one at the top instead of the people, the people become anemic and their spiritual gifts and muscles become atrophied. The structure must therefore reduce itself to the lowest common denominator in the pews, and Sunday morning becomes a ritual of entertainment and manipulation instead of empowerment and discipleship.

When we look at the world we see Hollywood, the music industry, and the political realm all built in pyramid fashion, with a few 'superstars' at the top. How sad it is that the 'church' looks just like them, a few 'royalty' at the top, and the impoverished multitude beneath.

Only in a flat structure can each gift be effectively developed. Only in a structure in which leadership submits to those it serves can each gift be empowered. Only in a structure that maintains relationships through mutual accountability can this happen, and this is the missing link.

Accountability

The question that remained while studying this was; what about accountability? If you get rid of the pyramid structure and empower everyone in a flat structure, who is in charge and how do you keep people from being too independent? Isn't this what pastors tell people who are thinking of starting their own work: "Who is your covering?" "Be careful; sounds like a cult." "Doing your own thing is how people get off." "I know people who really got burned by house church."

Character building forged in the midst of relationships.

Righteousness in Christ is designed to be worked out in the midst of relationships. It is within this context and understanding the New Testament was written, but is outside the thinking of most in the traditional church. Again the reason for this is because the pyramid does not foster relationships. It's all about the structure and program and person at the top. But within the context of the New Testament interpersonal and inter-generational relationships among family and friends in someone's living room and workplace were the norm, thus strong character was developed within these relationships.

Trying to maintain relationships within the pyramid structure is a very difficult thing to do because by its nature Jethro's pyramid discourages relationships outside the realm of that church's programs and service. Step outside the pyramid and there goes the relationships. Additionally, unless everyone in a traditional church has assigned seating, you may be sitting next to someone you either don't know, or only know from seeing them at church.

In house church we walk through life together, usually the same group of people are in the living room this week as they have been for the last several months. It means relationships develop and you help each other out in mutual growth in Christ.

This also means house church isn't spectacular nor will it tickle the ears. House church can be messy when you start developing relationships and conflict arises. The glue that holds it together is the willingness by all to continue going deeper into the things of God in terms of character building and becoming more Christ-like. Without the number one priority of being Christ-like in a house church, it will fall apart. That is everyone's focus.

Character supports the gifts and authority given to man

Because promotion in Jesus' government is downward to greater service, getting closer to the Cornerstone, becoming like Him, but upward in authority, it means these gifts and authority must be supported by proportionally greater character.

"Who in the days of his flesh, when he had offered up prayers and supplications with strong crying and tears to him that was able to save him from death, and was heard in that he feared; though he were a Son, yet he learned obedience by the things which he suffered." (Hebrews 5:7–8—KJV)

The closer Jesus got to the cross, the greater strength of character he had to develop and demonstrate. As we press toward our own 'cross', the same principle is true, especially for those at the bottom of the building closest to the Cornerstone. Even Jesus took his closest disciples to pray with him in Gethsemane. Though they slept, causing Jesus to ask if they couldn't even pray with him for one hour, Jesus was not alone during the time he was the most afraid and sweating blood.

Though I've been writing about giftings within each of us, those gifts are not what make us successful in life, nor Christian walk. It is always more fun to use our gifts, but it is character that supports the gifts. We love to hear a great singing voice, but that gift could not flow unless the person spent hours in private, practicing many hours for each 4 minute song performed.

The world does not care about character, it exalts the gift. Thus we have extremely gifted actors and actresses, musicians and writers who can't stay in a marriage relationship, or are perhaps in and out of rehabilitation for some addiction. We also have pastors, TV preachers, noted teachers and healers who have broken or damaged marriages, questionable lifestyles, and egos the size of Mt. Everest. The pyramid structure of church exalts the gift and authority, but requires no Christ-like character to stay on top.

When these gifts and character aren't growing alongside each other in balance a person can actually hide behind their gift—such as when a pastor excels in the pulpit but has been hiding an affair he's been having with a secretary. People who don't understand the Lord's process will want him back in the pulpit right away, but others will want to see a season proving character before letting him flow in his gift again.

When I was the pastor of a traditional church there was a man who wanted to become part of the worship team. We needed his gift for he could play a variety of instruments and would have added another dimension to the team, but he refused to come on Thursday nights for practice. He said he didn't need to pray and practice the songs for Sunday, because he was good enough he could just show up Sunday morning and pick it up.

He was right, he was that good. But Thursday night prayer and practice was about more than just knowing what songs were going to be sung three days later, it was about building unity and camaraderie in the worship team that was equally important for enhancing the worship experience.

Asking him to come Thursday nights involved developing character, and he didn't relish that. He just wanted to flow in the gift. Every person loves elements of their job, but each job has other parts that don't come naturally, and it is in those elements where God forges character to support the gifts.

Peter said it this way:

"For this very reason make every effort to supplement your faith with virtue, and virtue with knowledge, and knowledge with self-control, and self-control with steadfastness, and steadfastness with godliness, and godliness with brotherly affection, and brotherly affection with love. For if these things are yours and abound, they keep you from being ineffective or unfruitful in the knowledge of our Lord Jesus Christ." (II Peter 1:5–8 Revised Standard)

All these issues are character issues. Paul exhorted the Ephesians similarly:

"…throw off your old evil nature…stop lying to each other; tell the truth…if you are angry don't sin by nursing your grudge…if anyone is stealing he must stop it and begin using those hands of his for honest work…don't use bad language…stop being mean, bad-tempered and angry…instead be kind to each other…" (Eph 4:22–32 Living)

Consider that we esteem Paul as the greatest of the apostles—why? It is because he walked in his gifts and call to the fullest extent he could, coupled with his great service and character. We admire his character as much as glean from his wisdom!

When he wrote to Timothy and outlined qualities to look for in leadership in I Timothy 3, he outlined character and did not even mention gifts. Character supports gifts.

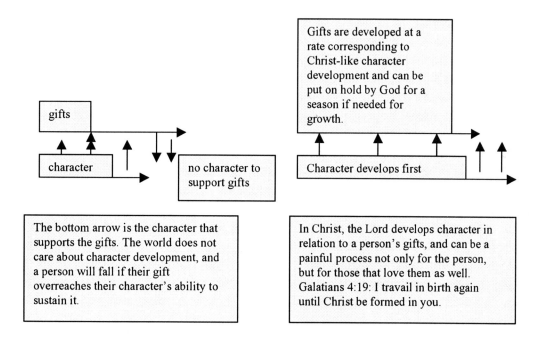

External control or internal control?

Jethro's pyramid of Exodus 18 was built to develop political control over its' people, issuing judgments and decisions to be enforced. This allowed leadership to maintain control over the people, but produced people who were incapable of making right decisions on anything but the most basic subjects, always having to go before a ruler above them to settle issues.

In the church pyramid it means the people aren't learning God's voice because only 1 person each week brings forth God's message, and the people rarely have close enough relationships in church to walk with them through the discipleship process, so many are incapable of governing themselves. This has created generations of people who are hearers only of the Word, content to come to church to be spoon fed each week, never venturing forth to develop themselves in their God-given gifts and character.

One of the greatest differences between the Jethro pyramid and the Biblical (apostolic) house church structure is that of humility. If an apostle or pastor sits atop a pyramid structure, it sets that person up for pride and competition much like Lucifer himself was lifted up 'because of his possessions'. The more territory you control, even if it is 50 people it may be quite an accomplishment for you, the more pride enters in.

By contrast, the true apostle realizes they are only one gift, one small part, of an overall body and they are at the bottom—furthermore they know they are on this planet to further God's kingdom, not their own.

Because they recognize their own giftings are of God and not of themselves, they can see God's grace at work in others as well. When they see that <u>everyone is equal</u> in their graces, <u>but with different functions</u> (Rom 12:3–4) they walk humbly, seeking to serve and develop those graces in others. Thus, they fulfill Jesus' command to submit to those they serve.

Jesus expects each person to learn to hear the voice of the Spirit, live responsibly, be accountable to one another in mutual submission, and flow together. "By your love they will know you."

The pyramid requires <u>control from the outside</u> and not giving a person authority. The house church requires the <u>inward recognition of the grace</u> in a person and giving them the freedom to move in it. The pyramid defeats relationships, the <u>house church can only flow</u> within relationships. The pyramid controls through fear, house church controls through relationships, honesty, love, and integrity, from within.

There is another element of tending the sheep from within that I noticed when I was a pastor in the traditional church, but now I've found works much better in the house church; and that is the ability to pastor supernaturally.

When I was a pastor in the traditional church my wife and I would be praying for members of our church and the Lord would often show us something about them or what they're going through or what He was trying to do in their lives. Because the nature of the relationship was contact with them limited to Sunday morning and maybe Wednesday night, we rarely felt the freedom to speak to them about what we were receiving.

In house church the depth of the relationships is greater, so not only do we get things in the Spirit for people in our church, but they get them for us, and they get things from God for each other. God's flow of revelation interconnects us all, versus in the pyramid where revelation flows only from the pulpit out to the congregation. It's not now unusual for any one of us to call, email, or visit each other without hesitation to inquire about what we think we're receiving from the Lord.

Apostles and leadership are mutually submitted to each other and the ones they serve. As Paul and Barnabas went to Jerusalem to have the leaders there speak into their lives, so too in house church does everyone speak into each other's lives. In Acts 21:4 we see disciples urging Paul not to go to Jerusalem and before them Paul mentioned wherever he went the Spirit (through disciples) was witnessing that trouble lay ahead. People could speak into Paul's life even as he spoke into theirs.

Jesus built the church that each gift would be recognized in its place in the body as a whole, and through the interdependence and relationships within the body, control would be by the body and through the Holy Spirit.

Remember that the letters of the New Testament were written to the whole church, not the leadership, because the writers recognized the 'ekklesia', the gathering of citizens for the purpose of conducting the business of the kingdom. Each member is mutually accountable, and so expected to take an active role. Order comes through understanding each person's gifting, with the accompanying respect and honor due.

When the Corinthian church had a case of one believer taking another to court, Paul told them to handle it as a body, setting those esteemed least to be judges. (I Cor 6:3–4)

> **"...Don't you know we will judge (rule over) angels? How much more things that pertain to this life? If you then have judgments...set them to judge who are least esteemed in the church (house church)." (NKJV)**

Paul expected them to take care of it as a body. Today in a traditional church, a ruler over 10 would pass it to a ruler over 50 who would pass it on up the line.

When they had a man in their midst who had entered into a sexual relationship with his stepmother, he told them they should have handled it as a body. (I Cor 5:2)

> **"...and you are puffed up and have not mourned, that he who has done this might be taken away from you." (KJV)**

Not once in chapters five or six, where these incidents are mentioned, did he ever call upon the elders or other leaders to step in. In chapter 11 he dealt with the issue of veils—and he never appealed to leadership. In chapters 12–14 dealing with the gifts, confusion, order and love, he never appealed to leadership to take control.

Furthermore, in Galatians where the issue was legalism, he never wrote to leadership…and even to The Revelation and the letters to the 7 churches—not once were any of them addressed to the leaders on those churches.

Paul taught responsible Christianity, Body governed as each person moves in his or her own grace.

We must recognize that God moves through the gifts he gave to the church. Gifts are what makes each person unique, it's who they are. <u>You cannot value and empower a gift separate from valuing and empowering the person</u>. To do this you must know them. Each of us is a gift to each other.

Chapter 9

Freedom to Flow

Relationships

Jesus told the disciples to teach **'them to observe and to do whatsoever I've commanded you'**. Jesus commanded and taught his disciples while living among them. Paul told Timothy to impart these things 'to faithful men' (II Tim 2:2), older women to the younger, older men to the younger, parents to children. It's all relationship based.

Only in relationships can we have the V or flat structure Jesus taught. Someone said that Christianity started as a relationship when God reached out to man in Israel; it went to Greece and became a philosophy, to Rome and became a religion, to Europe to become a culture, and to the United States to become an enterprise.

<u>Control is not an issue when people have the freedom to develop their gifts in Christ and are given a place to function within mutually accountable relationships.</u>

That doesn't mean there are never any problems, but it means through commitment to each other, maturity is attained.

In house church and relationship based Christianity; the degree to which a person grows is directly proportional to how much they want to grow, and often is dependent on the depth and quality of relationships they have with others. As mentioned above, the pyramid controls from the outside, urging people to get involved with various programs and be there at every service linking involvement in the church to spiritual growth.

The truth is, no matter how busy a person may be in a church, if they don't want to grow, if they don't want to apply the Word to their life, they won't grow. House church with strong relationships provides the environment which is best suited for growth.

In many traditional church bookstores today we can find material about growing in Christ. Much of it will center on righteousness, the new creation, and so forth, which are all good topics, but notice that rarely does it mention the New Testament practice of having close interpersonal relationships that help us walk out our salvation! Those that do focus on relationships are usually books on mentors, which is what develops naturally in a house church, but must be a determined effort in the pyramid.

The breakdown of the family and society, not to mention just plain old human nature, have produced people who don't know right from wrong, how to conduct themselves among others, and parents without parenting skills or discernment.

As I was helping to restructure a Bible school several years ago I made calls on various educators in that city. One told me that leaders in higher education had made some startling discoveries recently, including that young people were coming into higher education without any knowledge of social skills. Colleges were holding classes on skills such as ethics and etiquette, including how to conduct oneself during a job interview, how to organize a notebook, and how to talk to members of the opposite sex.

He concluded: "Things that used to be taught around the dinner table each night are no longer being taught, because the family has largely broken down and there is no family dinner table any longer. So the educational system has to try to fill in the gaps."

As I studied the pyramid versus house church, I had only to look around me to see the traditional church had made very little impact on society as a whole. What if the billions of dollars spent each year on buildings and programs had instead been invested in the lives of the congregation—paying mortgages, car payments, tuition, putting food on tables and heat in homes—instead of paying for huge edifices that denote one pyramid as being different than the pyramid down the road?

At the same time I realized that a house church structure such as employed in the New Testament could provide the sense of family and the ability to help in physical needs and impart life skills and wisdom to its members.

Growth in house church therefore has been demonstrated to be from the grass roots, growth in the pyramid is from the top down. Disciples are truly made, not born, and the pattern demonstrated in scripture is to accomplish this through close knit relationships centered on homes and families.

Freedom to be you

Notice the lack of top down control exhibited in Acts in the way people were allowed to do what they felt the Lord was leading them to do. It was really nothing more than people feeling led in a particular way, then talking through what they felt they were to do so that all the ramifications of their actions were taken into account.

In Acts 15 several representatives from Jerusalem, namely Paul, Barnabas, Barsabas, and Silas (Acts 15:22) are sent to Antioch with letters telling them they won't have to obey the Laws of Moses. After they had been in Antioch for awhile verses 32 and 34, 35 say:

> **"...And Judas and Silas, being prophets themselves exhorted the brethren...and after they had stayed for a space, they were released from the brethren to return to the apostles...Notwithstanding it pleased Silas to abide there still...Paul also and Barnabas continued in Antioch..." (KJV)**

Judas and Silas clearly wanted to get back to Jerusalem, but stayed until everyone agreed to let them go if they wished, however Silas decided to stay on as well as Paul and Barnabas. There was no top down ordering what to do; and the recognition of their gifts by the statement 'being prophets themselves' illustrates that in the final analysis, the brethren in Antioch trusted Christ in these men, thus giving them the blessing to leave if desired. It's clearly mutual submission and respect for each other's giftings guided by love.

I have to perceive God's grace in you and trust where Christ in you is leading. The flip side is that you are expected to respect me equally, giving me the same benefit of the doubt you want me to give you, thus we both walk in love. That is what these men practiced and what Peter did for Paul as mentioned earlier by perceiving the grace in him, while not understanding completely his call.

A house church has people gifted in many areas, and some of those gifts naturally conflict with each other, but are needed for the purpose of overall balance in the body. Some people have to learn that doing things differently than they would do them is not necessarily wrong, it's just different. Disciples in Christ who are pressing to maturity work through these differences and learn to appreciate the elements of God's personality in others instead of severing a relationship with those people. In the traditional church someone would leave and start attending church elsewhere, in house church you work through differences.

Conflict Resolution

In Acts 15: 36–41 we have a good look at conflict within the flat structure. Two men who are at the bottom right next to the Cornerstone are having an argument. Acts 13:1 said there were certain "prophets and teachers" and then names

Barnabas and Paul in that number. From that point they are called by the Holy Spirit to go out, thus they have been promoted downward to apostles. Right next to the Cornerstone, but they are having a heated argument.

On their first trip to start churches they took Barnabas' nephew John Mark along as their helper (Acts 13:5; Col 4:10), but he left them less than 1/3 of the way into the trip, and headed back home to Jerusalem (13:13). You may recall from Acts 12:12 that his mother Mary was hosting the prayer meeting in their house when Peter was released from prison by the angel. He ran back home to momma.

In Acts 15:36 Paul said:

"Let us go again and visit our brethren in every city where we have preached the word of the Lord and see how they are doing." (KJV)

Barnabas was determined to take John Mark with them, giving him a second chance, but Paul was dead set against it. He didn't want to get out there in some strange country only to have to take care of the kid or have him run off on them again.

If we examine this in light of a person manifesting the Spirit through their gifts as I Corinthians 12:7 says, then the situation becomes very clear. Barnabas' real name was Joses, but the apostles gave him the name of Barnabus in Acts 4:36, because Barnabus means 'comfort'. That verse also says he was a Levite from Cyprus. Barnabas was a peacemaker, one who brought comfort and consolation to others. This was his primary gift, or means by which God moved through him to manifest that aspect of His personality.

We first see him manifesting God's personality of comforter or peacemaker in Acts 9:26–27 where he boldly got to know Saul/Paul:

"And when Saul had come to Jerusalem, he wanted to join himself to the disciples: but they were all afraid of him and didn't believe he was a disciple. But Barnabas took him, and brought him to the apostles, and declared to them how he had seen the Lord in the way, and that he had spoken to him, and how he had preached boldly at Damascus in the name of Jesus." (NKJV)

Notice that Paul wanted to go to them, but no one believed him except Barnabas. Barnabas was risking his life getting to know Paul, willing to hear his side of the story, willing to check on what he did in Damascus. Armed with these reports and having taken the chance of getting to know Paul on his own, he introduced him to the leaders.

This example of Barnabas doing what was in him to do, is God moving in this situation to bring reconciliation. He manifested a facet of God's personality and that is how the Lord worked through him to bring the two sides together.

The next time we see him is Acts 11: 19–30. The situation is that very quickly on the heels of the Roman Centurion Cornelius' household turning to the Lord in Acts 10, reports of a great number of non-Jews receiving Jesus as Lord in the city of Antioch reaches the apostles in Jerusalem. This is very much a concern for the (Jewish) leadership in Jerusalem. The report is that non-Jews from Cyprus and Cyrene (Libya) and Greeks are turning to the Lord as well.

"Then rumors of this came to the ears of the church (assembly) in Jerusalem, and they sent Barnabas to Antioch." (Acts 19:22—AMP)

Why did they send Barnabas? Because they recognized his gifting, that element of God's personality in him (which is peacemaker and comforter) was needed in this potentially explosive situation. As would be revealed later in Acts 14 and 15, there was a faction in Jerusalem that either didn't believe non-Jews could be saved, or if they were, they must obey the Laws of Moses. It is a very controversial subject at this time.

Verses 23–24 go on to say of Barnabas:

"Who, when he came and saw the grace of God, was glad, and exhorted them all that with purpose of heart they should cleave to the Lord. For he was a good man and full of the Holy Spirit and of faith, and many people were added to the Lord." (KJV)

It is apparent that everyone was tense to have an emissary from Jerusalem. The statement of his character, that they found him to be a good man, was a huge relief to them all. They were accepted by Barnabas, and that meant they were accepted by the apostles as well.

But his gift doesn't stop manifesting there. He realizes they need teaching in the ways of the Lord, and seeing that they are Gentiles, he remembers that Paul was told by the Lord on the road to Damascus that he was called to the Gentiles. (Acts 26:17)

Verses 25–26 say this:

"Then Barnabas departed to Tarsus to look for Saul (Paul): And when he had found him, he brought him to Antioch. And it came to

pass that for a whole year they assembled themselves with the church, and taught many people. And the disciples were first called Christians in Antioch." (KJV)

Barnabas has not only been sent into a tense situation by the apostles and manifest the facet of God's personality of comfort and peacemaker within him once, but then he recognizes Paul's gift and gives him the opportunity to start being used by the Lord in that facet given to him.

We next see this aspect of God's personality in him in Acts 15, where he heatedly insists on taking his nephew John Mark with them to give him a second chance at success.

Though he introduced Paul to the apostles in Acts 9, and he opened the door for Paul in Acts 11, Paul insists this is not a situation where Barnabas' particular gift is going to manifest. Paul was not about to give Mark a second chance.

"...And the contention was so sharp between them, that they separated one from the other: and so Barnabas took Mark, and sailed to Cyprus; and Paul chose Silas and departed..." (Acts 15:39–40— KJV)

In the pyramid thinking we would think a friendship has ended. The cliché "agree to disagree" has been used in traditional circles to signify the end of a friendship, a kind of truce in which no relationship can exist after that truce has been agreed to. But we must look at this passage in light of the context of house church and the manifestation of facets of God's personality through these men.

First, Paul is completely right. But then again, Barnabas is completely right. Huh? Barnabas rightly saw potential in John Mark and wanted to develop that just as he had done with Paul. Paul was right in that the practical needs and stresses of a long trip required commitment that John Mark had previously backed away from. To repeat the same mistake twice would have been ludicrous.

Paul is concerned for the practical issues and wanted Barnabas to see his point. Barnabus was concerned about heart issues and wanted Paul to see his point. Both manifestations of these gifts are manifestations of the Holy Spirit (I Cor 12:7). God is concerned for the practical and He is also concerned with the heart.

In the flat structure of house church relationships both gifts are allowed to manifest. The real thing that happened here is that a determination was made that it was time for each gift to go its separate way. They did not agree to disagree, but rather agree that each was right and they empowered each other to do what was right for them.

Paul was proven right in that it was he and Silas that were beaten and left hanging in chains in the Philippian jail, not Paul, John Mark, and Barnabas. John Mark most certainly would have left them once again.

But Barnabas is proven right as well, for after going to their home country of Cyprus, giving John Mark time to examine his life and his failure as Paul's assistant, he returned to Jerusalem and became Peter's assistant, traveling all the way to Rome with him. Additionally, it was from the lips of Peter that John Mark wrote the gospel of Mark, finally finding his place in the work of God. In fact, in that gospel he points out his earlier tendency to run when the going gets tough in Mark 14:51–52 when Jesus is arrested in the Garden.

"…And there followed him a certain young man, having a linen cloth cast about his naked body; and the young men laid hold on him: And he left the linen cloth, and fled from them naked." (KJV)

Bible scholars are agreed that in the style of writing in that time, this young man would most certainly have been the author, John Mark. He ran in the Garden, he ran on his first trip, but thanks to Barnabas, a man with a gift for finding peace and comfort, he moved into his ministry as Peter's assistant.

In the pyramid structure we would think that those relationships were lost. But if we 'perceive the grace' that is in each of us, realizing these are elements of God's personality within each of us, we just agree that our gifts must go their separate ways for a time, yet we hold onto the person.

In II Timothy 4:11 Paul tells Timothy to bring John Mark "for he is profitable for the ministry". Paul and Barnabas are also teamed after this argument for in I Corinthians 9:6 he asks them if he and Barnabas have the authority (as apostles) to not work regular jobs, but instead earn their living from the gospel.

As severe as the break up of the ministry team of Paul and Barnabas appears on the surface, when understood within the context of house church and Jesus' structure instead of the pyramid, we see it not as a severing of relationships, just a temporary decision to let those gifts manifest separately. In house church two people can agree to disagree but remain friends and co-workers. In the pyramid more often than not, the relationship is lost.

It could also be noted that in Acts 16:1–3 Paul picks up a young man named Timothy as his assistant and co-worker. Again, Paul recognizes the grace in this young man. In Acts 17:14–15 Paul allows Silas and Timothy to stay at Berea for a while, and later asks them to come join him. Would that have been Barnabas and John Mark instead of Silas and Timothy had things been different? We don't know, but God, flowing through Himself in people and therefore His gifts within people, was orchestrating things in the big picture so everyone entered into their individual destinies.

Biblical, and therefore house church leadership recognizes the grace of God in a person, and whether they understand it or not, trusts God in that person and allows them to flow in their gift through mutual submission and respect.

Chapter 10

The Good, the Bad, and the Ugly Ways of Doing House Church

Nobody in charge during a meeting?

As I considered God moving through the gifts we are to each other coupled with the development of character within the ekklesia meeting in small home based churches, I became aware of all the varieties of house churches in the west today. Having a sound scriptural understanding of the New Testament however makes it easy to spot those that are off balance or perhaps not complete in their understanding.

One element in some house church circles is the segment that doesn't believe there should be any leader designated in a meeting.

Like the Friends or Quakers, they advocate everyone waiting on the Lord and then anyone who has something share it with the group. While there is little doubt that such meetings are a part of the mix, especially prayer meetings, it is clear in the New Testament that there were leaders in charge of nearly every meeting.

When Paul states in I Corinthians 14:26 that when they come together any may have a song of worship, teaching, revelation or moving of the gifts of the Spirit, if taken by itself without any overall view of the New Testament it could sound like no one is in charge. But the context of that passage is order, politeness and cultural considerations.

Paul said in 14:6:

"…what shall I profit you except I speak to you by revelation, knowledge, prophesying or doctrine…?" (KJV)

In other words, he was going to have something to give them, he wasn't going to wait while they all sat in silence waiting for someone to get something from the Lord. It would not profit them unless he had something to share.

Do we see any example in the lives of Jesus, Paul, Peter, or other person in the gospels or Acts in which they were part of a meeting that no one was in charge? Each time Jesus went somewhere he had something to say. The same could be said of the apostles.

There are three examples in Acts of meetings in which no one was in charge. One example is Acts 2:1 when 120 people gathered 'in one accord' to seek the Lord and Pentecost ensued. Another is when a house full of people is praying for Peter in Acts 12:12 and he was released from prison miraculously, and the other example is Acts 13:2 where it lists at least five men gathered to seek the Lord:

"...As they ministered to the Lord, and fasted, the Holy Spirit said, 'Separate unto me Barnabus and Saul for the work whereunto I have called them..." (KJV)

Clearly this was a meeting where they were collectively seeking the Lord to see what he would say. There are meetings like this today of course. Even in a regular house church meeting the leader may tell everyone they really didn't get any direction from the Lord so they will all worship and pray to see what the Lord says.

There is nothing wrong with this of course; the error comes when someone says this is the ONLY way to do it. The truth is that it's just a small part of the mix.

Throughout the gospels and Acts, wherever the narrative takes us and whomever it focuses on, that person had meetings where they knew what God wanted to say to the people. From John the Baptist to Jesus to Paul to Peter, the gift to the people was in part, what they had to say.

As I said, gifts are who people are, and as I Corinthians 12:7 says, each of them is a manifestation of the Spirit. Therefore I came to understand that the best house church structure seemed to have leaders who were also often the hosts like Lydia, Nymphas, Philemon, Jason, Justus, Crispus or Priscilla and Aquila, who were in charge of the meeting that day in their homes.

I could now see in scripture how the practice of letting God set the agenda was balanced by Paul's instruction concerning order and politeness as guests in someone's house, within the context of the clear indication that the hosts of the meeting were in charge.

In his letters we see Paul regularly greeting those named above and including in his greeting to them: "and the church in your house." The leaders were ultimately responsible for letting God have his way in the meeting, whether that meant flowing through them, or someone else, by meeting in their homes they were seen as the authority in those meetings.

Remembering that God manifests facets of his personality through each of us according to how he has gifted us, it means a person leading with gifting for prayer, will take the meeting in that direction. A person gifted in music will have that element of God's personality manifest. A teacher will teach and an exhorter may have a time of sharing testimonies; no two meetings are alike because the Lord will choose to bring forth what he wants within the mix of those present at each meeting. It is not a sin or unscriptural to have someone in charge of a meeting, in fact having someone in charge who has the maturity to be led of the Lord can actually facilitate God accomplishing his purpose for that meeting, in part because they know when to talk and when to be quiet.

For these reasons I came to understand that though there are meetings in which nobody has a specific direction, the overwhelming evidence in scripture is that someone was ultimately in charge in house church, usually the hosts and hostesses.

From just a social aspect, even if church is held in someone's home and someone other than the host or hostess leads that meeting, if there is a question about which direction to go, whoever is in charge should defer to the host or hostess.

I started a house church network called The Church Without Walls International (CWOWI), and in our Tulsa house churches it is not unusual for people wanting to hang around a bit or perhaps go out to eat if we aren't having a potluck that day. As a host or hostess, there could be a concern about people 'hanging around' all afternoon if they would prefer to rest or had something to do. Therefore any decision becomes subject to the host or hostess' wishes.

We usually rotate houses each week so the burden of hosting church isn't on any one family's shoulders, and each host has the right to either lead a meeting or request that someone else take it, though the meeting is in their home. There are some CWOWI affiliates that are held primarily in one home every week but rotating leadership helps ease the burden.

But always, unless the person in charge feels led another way, they are responsible for spending enough time with the Lord to get clear direction, at least enough to start a meeting.

I say that because there have been times the leader just says they didn't get anything and it becomes a meeting like in Acts 13:1–3. Other times they may say that but someone else has the direction for the meeting.

House church is flexible for our goal is for the Lord to have His way and His will in anything we do, and allowing the diversity of giftings resident in all the people makes for no two meetings alike.

Women and house church

I'd like to address an issue found in some circles of house church and that is women are not allowed to participate during meetings. They believe they are following Paul's instructions in I Corinthians 14 and I Timothy 2, but are in fact in error, not understanding the scriptural context and cultural issues of the day.

In Paul's first letter to the Corinthians, a church that met in the homes of Justus and Crispus (and others) Paul gives instruction concerning the wearing of veils by married women who are praying and/or prophesying (11:5). Twice Paul asks them to judge in themselves or consider the customs of that region, and to do what is right accordingly. (v11:13, 16)

When reading this passage we must understand the context of many couples meeting in the living rooms, dining rooms, courtyards and atriums of various homes of that age and style in and around Corinth, with some of the women discovering their freedom in Christ and choosing not to wear their veils, thus setting up heated discussions in homes throughout the city.

It should be noted that the issue was not whether they should be speaking, that is praying and prophesying in the meetings, but rather whether they should be veiled when doing so. In our day and age those that conduct house churches in which women are not allowed to speak misunderstand the passage—the issue isn't the praying and prophesying—it's whether they are properly clothed for the local culture while praying and prophesying.

In that culture, for a married woman not to wear her veil—a sign of submission and revealing publicly her status as a married woman—was an act dishonoring her husband, and could make the woman look at the least like she was single and at the worst a prostitute if someone saw her and did not understanding her freedom in Christ.

Can you imagine the debate about whether to wear veils or not? Yes we can because in our day and age in the west some churches have debated make up, length of skirts, hair style, ear and body piercing, tattoos, and other cultural issues. Even in American culture, a married woman generally wears her wedding ring, while the husband may or may not. In my generation, if a married woman is not wearing her wedding band it raises questions. In the predominantly Moslem cultures where the Burkha is considered normal attire for a woman, if a woman suddenly became a disciple of Christ and decided to remove her veil it could mean her death!

How important was the veil during Paul's time? In their time, at that place in time, the wearing of a veil was like a wife wearing a wedding ring for a wife in the west today, and much more. Thus Paul instructs them to obey the custom and wear the sign of their marriage, the veil. They could speak and prophesy in the meetings, just properly clothed for the customs of that age and time.

Paul's appeal to obey the local customs even though they know their freedom from such things in Christ, serves as a guiding principle for cultural decisions today.

For instance, when I've led numerous groups to ministry trips in Mexico, the custom is for the women to wear skirts below the knee to a service. They may be free in Christ and in the US they could wear whatever they wanted, but the custom of Mexico is for knee length or longer skirts.

The fact that Paul is appealing to cultural issues is not only proven by reading the passage within context, but simply by looking around you and asking if it is expected of Christian women today around the world to wear veils (as is custom in the Moslem world?) The answer is no, we understand as most of 2,000 years worth of Christians have understood it as a cultural issue for that day and time, but we glean the principles in Paul's instructions by which to make similar cultural decisions today.

The issue in I Corinthians 11:2–16 wasn't whether the wives and women should pray or prophesy, it was what they were wearing when they were praying and prophesying. Paul's instructions were to dress according to the custom of the day; it's that simple.

Social etiquette concerning the gifts of the Spirit; and should women keep quiet?

Just as Paul dealt with social etiquette concerning the wearing of veils in a house church setting in chapter 11, later in chapter 14 he address other social issues. In I Cor 14:26–33 Paul writes some guidelines for the way a meeting should be conducted.

In verse 26 he says this:

> **"How is it <u>brethren</u>? When you meet together, each one of you has a hymn (worship), lesson (doctrine—a teaching), a revelation (a new thing the Lord has shown you), a tongues or interpretation (the moving of the Gifts of the Spirit) let all be done for edification." (Revised Standard)**

Paul is addressing "brethren" and Vine's Dictionary of NT Words brings out the fact that the word 'brethren' may refer to men only, but based on context also means men and women. Considering his opening greeting was "to the church of God which is at Corinth, to them that are sanctified in Christ Jesus" (1:2) we can see he is addressing men and women together in his letter, thus his use of 'brethren' in this passage clearly includes women.

Additionally, understanding that the churches at Corinth met in the households of at least two people we know, Crispus and Justus, when he says; "when <u>you meet together</u> **every one of you** has…" we understand he is talking to everyone—men and women together. He is saying that everyone may participate and everything done in the meeting will naturally fall under one of these categories—worship, teaching, revelation, gifts of the Spirit.

After listing areas of participation in verse 26, Paul proceeds to give some guidelines, which are really just basic social courtesies which anyone would follow if they were a guest in someone's home, as they were:

> **If anyone speaks in a (strange) tongue, let the number be limited to two or at the most three, and each one (taking his) turn, and let one interpret and explain (what was said). (v27—AMP)**

Notice that his instruction to limit the moving of a single gift to two or three people and telling them (and us) to take turns is nothing more than exhorting them to be courteous and non-dominating, for they are guests in a larger meeting in someone's home. He continues in this vein in verses 28–30:

> **"But if there is no one to interpret, let him be quiet and speak to himself, and to God. So, let two or three prophets speak—those inspired to preach or teach—while the rest pay attention and weigh and discern what is said. And if anything is revealed to someone sitting near, let the first one hold his peace." (AMP)**

Notice again, he's just stating basic social courtesy that is required when you are a guest in someone's home. Essentially he is saying, "If you feel you have a word from the Lord, but there is no opportunity, then keep quiet and speak it to yourself". And in verses 29 & 30 he is saying to take turns, deferring to one another.

It's not a sin to get a word from the Lord and not give it. This comes as a huge revelation for some, and for the person used to insisting they give their word, it runs contrary to what they think. But it is scripture. In our society people become all lifted up with their own self importance, demanding that they be allowed to give the word God gave them for someone even if they have to pave the way themselves. That is rude and exactly what scripture is addressing here. Paul is trying to protect against people dominating a meeting, as can happen in home based meetings, so he says to take turns and defer to one another in an orderly fashion.

You do this all the time and don't even realize it. When you are thinking about someone and praying for them when you are alone, often the Lord will give you impressions or words of knowledge about them or their situation, and all you do is lift it up in prayer. You don't run to that person and tell them what you sensed or think the Lord showed you in prayer, you keep it to yourself as a matter of prayer. Then if the opportunity arises later you may share with them what you felt you received for them. You follow basic rules of courtesy and love.

Similarly, when there is group prayer with everyone taking turns lifting up various people and issues, or when we are praying for someone sitting in a chair with several people laying hands on them, everyone is sensitive to take turns and not to cut off someone else.

The same rules apply when you come together in house church. If you get a word, but there isn't the time or flow or it's not good manners to share it, keep it between you and the Lord.

The instruction of "**letting the others judge**" serves notice that if you give a word it is subject to everyone's opinion in the meeting, but what Paul states is really nothing more than social courtesy. With the open format of verse 26 of having everyone sharing, there must also be <u>mutual accountability</u> or else confusion will reign, and that is Paul's concern in this passage. The dominating person wants to talk, but they don't like their 'word' questioned. He tells them if you share then others have the right to scrutinize it and you don't have the right to be offended if they do.

That also means if a person doesn't want you to lay hands on them for prayer or doesn't want you to give them what you think God has shown you for them, they may refuse your request and word. No one has the right to violate basic social courtesies, which are based on what Paul wrote the previous chapter on love—love doesn't push itself forward nor insist on its own way—and that certainly applies to a meeting in the home.

I have been in house church meetings where one person insists on reading something or giving a word even though the consensus of the group is to move on. I've seen married men habitually seek out single women only to give them a word in private. There are other times where one person dominates the meeting, droning on for 45 minutes without letting a person get a word in edge-wise. If these people were taught and understood the passages above within their context, they would mind social courtesies. Many times people want to have their say but don't want to be held accountable. Paul tells them they may all speak—in order and in turn—but the flip side is whatever they say may be judged by the others as being from God or not. In verse 32 Paul says:

"The spirits of the prophets are subject to the prophets." (KJV)

Again, Paul is saying that you may feel you have to give that word, but in fact, what you have in your spirit is subject to you. You don't have to give that word if there is no interpreter, or someone to 'bounce it off of' to be sure it's right on, or if the timing is wrong. Paul concludes in verse 33 saying that **God is not the author of confusion, but of peace**…and he wants a home church meeting to be dominated by peace, not confusion.

So what do you do? Realize that the person who dominates lacks social skills for a reason. Either emotional issues, fresh from a hurting situation in their lives, self-image, or some other reason, they need tolerance and understanding at first. When the time comes, Paul said to instruct people in meekness (Gal 6:1).

When you instruct them one of two things will happen; either they will accept it, or they will be offended and leave. We've found that when a house church follows the basic social courtesies Paul set forth, these guidelines don't allow a person to manifest a dominating manner, and they either grow into maturity in this area or leave.

You don't want to pounce on someone if you feel they are dominating or flaky, but as a leader you may need to step in and redirect the meeting. Remember that house church is based on relationships. Therefore wait, be patient, look for God's timing. Don't look for the slightest wrong, but look for progress in their lives.

Scripture indicates the foundational rules for conducting meetings in the home rests upon social courtesies. Someone who dominates a meeting isn't walking in love, for love doesn't push itself forward or insist on having its own way (13:4–8). Make sure you address the issue in love, showing them the way.

Immediately after he tells them that the spirits of the prophets are subject to the prophets and that God is not the author of confusion, but of peace, he says this in v34–35:

"Women (wives) should be silent during the church meetings. They are not to take part in the discussion, for they are subordinate to men as the Scriptures also declare. (Gen 3:16—parenthesis mine) If they have any questions to ask, let them ask their husbands at home, for it is improper for women to express their opinions in church meetings." (Living)

Taken by itself this passage would seem to tell women to be completely silent during meetings. But the first rules of Biblical interpretation include setting the context by asking who is this written for and under what conditions and customs? Another rule is to look at other writings by the same author or elsewhere in scripture to gain balance.

In I Corinthians 11:5 Paul mentions that women are praying and prophesying—with or without a veil, and we've noted his acceptance of women in ministry, so why would he mention women praying and prophesying in chapter 11 and then tell them to be quiet in chapter 14?

Because the context in this passage, from verse 26 where he says all may participate in worship, teaching, revelation and the gifts, through this verse has to do with orderliness, peace, and social courtesies while conducting meetings as guests in someone's home. The Law doesn't tell the wives to be quiet; it says they are subject to their husbands, for Eve was drawn from Adam. Even Abraham, the father of the faith, submitted to and obeyed Sarah in Genesis 16:2.

Paul mentions this same issue of women and orderliness in meetings when he writes Timothy in Ephesus. In I Timothy 2:9–10 he encourages the women to dress appropriately, a cultural issue again for he tells them not to wear gold or pearls, nor to braid their hair. Today it is accepted as normal in most cultures for women to fix their hair in different styles and to wear gold and pearls.

He goes on to say in v11:

"Women (wives) should listen and learn quietly and humbly. I never let women teach men or lord it over them. Let them be silent in your church meetings. Why? Because God made Adam first, and afterwards made Eve." (Living)

Again, this is in context of Paul's instruction about cultural issues of dress and jewelry, and his concern is about wives usurping authority over the husbands.

Going back to the Spirit and the Word agreeing, we must examine what the Spirit of God is doing in the world, and then verify it in the Word of God. I've already mentioned Joyce Meyer and Marilyn Hickey in our time and could mention many more. If we went back through the corridors of church history we could mention Kathryn Kuhlman, Aimee Semple McPherson, Joan of Arc, Madame Guyon , and so forth.

So if God is against women speaking, then why has he anointed so many not only today, but down through the ages, not to mention Paul's own ministry partners? How can the Spirit and the Word agree on this subject? The answer is context. In two brief passages, I Corinthians 14:35 and I Timothy 2:12, Paul states that to avoid confusion in meetings and/or be sure a wife is not usurping authority over her husband, he asks them to be quiet. The context of both is cultural issues and order in a meeting.

In Paul's day women were not allowed to be educated, and you can imagine the questions and confusion generated when the wives started sitting together in meetings with their husbands, asking their husbands all sorts of questions trying to catch up in knowledge—to avoid confusion for everyone Paul told them to ask their husbands later at their own homes, but to allow the meeting to go forward. That's all it was.

Miniature of the pyramid

Some house churches seem to be the home for a frustrated preacher who never got a pulpit. Instead of following the New Testament example of each person having something to contribute if they wish, this house church only becomes a miniature of the traditional church they left. Often promoting relationships or small group as the drawing card, attendees soon find it's nothing more than the usual Sunday morning pyramid small group style, and they rarely last for long.

I've even seen house churches in which the main leader calls upon people to make remarks, looking like a 6th grade class filled with reluctant students. In the end it was just like a pastor in the pyramid polling the congregation for comments about a sermon. There was no life or spontaneity and shortly failed.

There are times in a new house church filled with new believers that perhaps the hosts are the only mature Christians and for a time they will need to lead. However Paul included in the mix of I Corinthians 14:26 'revelation', meaning someone could share something the Lord has recently shown them. Also included were the gifts of the Spirit which are not based on maturity or knowledge.

One of the quickest ways to mature a house church is to rotate leaders each week, which makes the person in charge of next week get into the Word and prayer to get the mind of the Lord.

When we first started CWOWI in our home in Tulsa, we met twelve weeks in a row in our house. For the first six weeks I shared the concept of house church and other things the Lord put on my heart. While praying about what to share just before the sixth week the Lord spoke to me and said, "You've spoken enough, now delegate out and let someone else talk."

At the close of week six in our home I shared that someone else would need to lead next week—and they all looked like deer caught in head lights! They just stared at me batting their eyes, but finally one young man spoke up and offered to lead next week. What he shared was excellent and blessed everyone. Now we generally follow the practice of whoever is hosting is the leader, though often the host may want someone else to lead while they focus on just hosting a group of people in their home that week.

Focus on one doctrine

One house church was doing fine until three or four members attended an inner healing conference. From that point on the whole focus of the church became everyone's need for inner healing, and the group dissolved.

I've seen house churches built around personal prophesy, inner healing, communion, meals, and much more. Balance is the key and as long as one particular doctrine is front and center balance is impossible.

At one house church conference a lively discussion revolved around communion as a bread and juice practice or communion as a larger meal. One group noted that the Last Supper was part of a larger meal that included lamb, herbs, bread and wine, and so celebrated communion as part of a larger pot luck meal. Others thought bread and juice should be served as a separate event during house church, then everyone could eat a regular meal afterwards.

The key is that house church can be flexible, as mentioned earlier, changing structure to follow life, and communion may be served in several ways. The key is not to get hung up on one doctrine and practice to the point there is no longer life, but only ritual remaining.

Reacting out of hurt

In studying various house churches I've found that a fair number of them follow pet doctrines out of hurt incurred while in the pyramid church structure. Some are very wary of leadership because they were burned by leaders in the traditional church. Others don't want any Charismatic gifts flowing because of either hurt, ignorance, or bad experience and teaching. Some believe that if a house church links up with another in some sort of network or association they have created a denomination, which is of course silly because all of Paul's letters were written to churches in his own network, but their experience within a denomination dictates how they do house church.

I have been in meetings where someone begins sharing how this church or that church hurt them, and it is sometimes hard to redirect a meeting when that happens, because we all have a story or two we could tell.

There was a time I had to be out of town for ministry and my wife felt led of the Lord to attend one of the house churches in our network in particular that Sunday morning. During the meeting a man started talking about how one particular denomination had hurt him, and the atmosphere in the living room immediately changed for the worse, as it often does when someone drags on about hurts or fears.

Before it went much further my wife stepped in and addressed the issue, telling everyone that though we've all experienced things in the traditional church, meeting in house church was not the place to dredge up old wounds. Those hurts were hurts of the heart and were therefore private in nature. If anyone would like to talk privately about their experiences with she or myself later for the purposes of forgiving, receiving healing, and moving on from those hurts we would be happy to do so in private with them. That ended the topic and they changed their focus back to the Lord and what he was doing in their lives, not on what the devil had done in the past.

Meeting on Sunday?

Meeting times vary within our network based on local customs and spiritual atmosphere. In Tulsa we had one church that met on Thursday nights and had a couple attending that went to a traditional church on Sunday mornings. They volunteered in the parking lot Sunday mornings helping direct traffic and assisting worshippers as well. One day the pastor stated from the pulpit that members of that church were expected to attend only that church and no others. This raise a huge conflict in the couple that was coming on Thursdays as you can imagine because they loved both Thursday nights with us (and got more out of it) but loved the vision of the church they attended on Sunday mornings.

They made the decision to obey that pastor and started going to that church's Wednesday night services instead of our Thursday night church. After that we decided that in Tulsa, the so called Buckle of the Bible belt, it would be better to meet on Sunday mornings.

However, the first weekend of the month we do something different. Sometimes we have a potluck after meeting, other times we do something else altogether different. We've gone bowling, gone to a restaurant, had a BBQ at a member's house, and more besides in lieu of meeting that week for church. We follow life and what everyone wants to do and it's fun.

Other house churches in our network meet weeknights or Sunday morning or afternoon, it varies by what is convenient and the local church culture.

Meeting with Purpose

Perhaps the most difficult time for a group of people who meet together on a regular basis is the time between coming out of the traditional pyramid and the time they decide to do church.

For the sake of example let's say there is a group of disciples gathering weekly on Friday nights after work and often involves a meal. There is worship, prayer, Bible study and sharing, and the time it breaks up varies depending on what everyone has going on the next day; it could be 8:30pm, it could last until midnight.

They are functioning as the ekklesia, the church, by caring for one another, taking care of each other's needs, walking through life's challenges together. But if talk of becoming a 'church' rises, fear and heated discussions follow. This is because of the ingrained doctrine of the pyramid system, which means 'church' has a context within that system, and no one wants to return to what they just came out of.

Like a couple living together and not wanting to ruin what they have by getting married because bad experiences in marriage warped their understanding of what it is, so too are these Bible studies not wanting to call themselves church because of bad experiences. Often they understand house church through the eyes of the traditional church, not knowing there was anything else, so they don't think they want it.

To call themselves 'church' would be launching into the unknown because they have no healthy examples of what church can be. Imagine going back to Paul's time and trying to explain a jet airplane. They have no point of reference in their understanding. Do you compare it to a man made bird? It flies like a bird, but bigger? How can a couple living together be convinced of the beauty and joy in marriage if they have no point of reference for a healthy one?

How can we describe what we are doing when the answer is right there in chapter & verse, but they can only understand those verses through the eyes of the pyramid?

Several house churches I know started because one or two families had de-churched themselves but still wanted to meet with other Christians on a regular basis. Over the course of more than a year it dawned on them that they were a church. They were the church, the ekklesia, but it took over a year to come to that realization, such was the pervasive nature of the pyramid structure. It's not unusual for one or even two years to pass before people start realizing they've left the church to become the church.

That said; there is a huge difference between just meeting as a Bible study among friends and meeting with the purpose of being a church. An informal meeting between friends requires no commitment to each other, no examination of purpose, and no examination of direction. There is a certain freedom and relaxation involved when there is no pressure to be a church; you can float in and out as your schedule requires and live life independently.

Nowhere in Acts do we see a church starting without purpose. Once believers gathered together they were the church, the ekklesia, eager to conduct the business of the kingdom, eager to grow deeper in the things of God. When Paul left preaching and teaching in the Synagogue of Corinth to meet in the homes of Justus (right next door) and Crispus they were committed to each other and doing God's work. It is written of Paul in Ephesus when persecution erupted, 'he departed from them and separated the disciples'. (Acts 19:9)

Have you become a church by accident? Do the members of your Bible study care for one another? Do you walk through life's hardships together seeking to grow in Christ at each turn? Does the Lord have his way in your meetings and needs get met? If the answers are yes, your little gathering may in fact have become a church. But because the word 'church' has connotations of a pyramid you haven't been able to find a term to describe what it is you do. Rest easy, you are doing church.

> **The labels may differ slightly, and the application will vary a bit, but the essential elements will remain the same, all founded upon Revelation from God, Purpose, and Commitment to each other in Relationship Based Christianity.**

Heretics?

If you are a student of church history you will realize a basic principle. **The previous move of God persecutes the current move of God**: As denominations persecuted and didn't understand the Charismatic Renewal (or movement), so too are the churches that rose up out of that Renewal/movement not understanding and/or persecuting house church. The difference is that because this 'movement' (I hesitate using that word) is actually the way they did church in the New Testament it is a movement that will not pass away. The family and God in the family and community started in the Garden of Eden. House church is not going away.

Many house churches start out as independent groups of individuals, couples and families who just want to worship and pray in a way where God sets the agenda and they can respond to each other's needs. But to the pyramid structure independence from a pyramid is heretical. A person or group of people must be willing to pay the price of persecution from people within a pyramid not understanding what you are doing.

I recently attended an 'apostolic' conference that included a workshop on house church. Their view of house churches was that they were all made up of people who were hurt and wounded, had no leadership, and the solution was to bring these people back under the authority of a large local church. They just didn't get it.

While there are some examples that resemble what they shared, overall that is not the case.

When sharing about house church with those in the traditional church we are using terms they know, but within a different context. Remember, the whole kingdom operates on revelation, and prayer for them and discussion with them is the best way to open a door for God to show them his Word.

Remember the transition time in Acts in which the church continued meeting in the temple area for a year or two, until Saul's persecution caused them all to leave the city (except the apostles). Remember how long God was stirring you to look elsewhere for spiritual satisfaction before you were willing to leave the pyramid. Be patient and allow God to work in them.

Chapter 11

Where Do I Go From Here?

The Person of Peace

The reader may be asking how do I start or get involved in house church. When Paul went about seeking disciples of Jesus he sought out a specific type of individual. The first people he went to were those who already believed in God. He didn't usually go to people who didn't know of the Jewish God unless it was a situation like on Mars Hill in Acts 17 when he could scarcely contain himself because of their idolatry.

In general practice Paul went to the synagogues of his day and taught Jesus. Once he had a few who believed he separated them and that started the church.

Starting a church is different than going into the highways and byways seeking converts to Christianity. Paul's approach wasn't like someone passing out tracts in a store parking lot and seeing who responds and taking the most stable of the bunch. He deliberately sought out people with a degree of stability in their lives to be his core group.

In Philippi, which didn't have a synagogue but had a Jewish population that met by the river for prayer (Acts 16:13–16), he met a single businesswoman named Lydia in what had to be a divine appointment. Her home and household became the core for the church in Philippi.

In Corinth he happened upon a couple named Aquila and Priscilla who were business owners and together with Paul discipled the newly converted ruler of the synagogue, a man named Crispus. We could later note that Philemon hosted a church in his house (Philemon 2) and that he was a slave owner as the letter to Philemon is all about the return of one Onesimus, now a brother in the Lord. That means that Philemon was a man of some substance as well. In Ephesus his base became a school owned by Tyrannus, which means that Tyrannus had some stability and maturity in his life.

In short, Paul followed the principle laid out by Jesus in Luke 10: 1–20 when he sent out the 70 as a sort of advance team. In verses 6–9 the text says of coming to a house:

> **"And if a son of peace is there, your peace shall rest upon him; but if not it shall return to you. And remain in the same house, eating and drinking what they provide, for the laborer deserves his wages; do not go from house to house….heal the sick in it." (Revised Standard)**

Paul looked for people of peace. What does that mean? From Paul's practice we see they were people who had a measure of peace in their lives. They were mature, had some life experience, and were stable.

Paul did not seek out those in transition in life nor families that were in disarray. Paul would further enlarge upon Jesus' instructions of a person of peace when he wrote Timothy in I Timothy 3 and described the character of potential leaders in the (house) churches in Ephesus. He was describing people of peace.

Our minds are entrenched with the pyramid's way of thinking in evangelism and church planting, which is exactly opposite the way Jesus taught and Paul practiced. Notice that when Jesus told the 70 to go into a home where a 'son of peace' lived, he told them to stay in that house, eat what they gave them, and heal the sick therein. He told them specifically not to jump from house to house, but to stay and get to know that family.

This is a different context than Acts 2:42–46 that states that once the house churches were started the people and apostles visited from house to house. Paul did the same in Acts 20:20 in Ephesus as well, and is therefore not in conflict. The context of Luke 10 is that of Jesus headed towards his death in Jerusalem and sending advance teams before him to multiply his efforts.

Our thinking in the traditional church was that Jesus sent the 70 to preach on every street corner and alley way they could find, but that again is transferring pyramid mentality to what was in Jesus' mind a house church strategy. He said to go to a house with a person of peace and STAY THERE. He specifically said to stay there with that family and heal the sick therein. From there they could expand outside that family to the village, but they were to use that home as a home base.

Thus when the 70 return rejoicing because even the demons were subject to the name of Jesus, they weren't saying it based on their experiences on street corners, alley ways and massive crusade-like crowds, they had those experiences in their host homes and neighborhoods! They stayed with that family of peace and brought the fullness of salvation to that household and then ministered out from there, but always staying at that house.

When I look around within our own network of house churches and outside our network, one common trait I see is that when there is a core of 'people of peace', that house church will be successful. This core group has a relative peace about their lives, though there are always issues in life, yet they have enough peace and stability to be able to manifest the hearts of leaders who care for the sheep.

Therefore, when contemplating starting a house church a person should take a good look at their life and the lives of those around them. I do believe every house church needs people in various stages of discipleship and therefore various levels of maturity in it, but the core group needs to be people of peace.

Share the load

Notice that when Lydia got saved, it was also her whole household (Acts 16:15). The same was said of the Philippian jailer (16:34). Paul teamed up with Aquila and Priscilla and Crispus and his whole household (18:8). Tyrannus had a school which meant he had a staff structure, and certainly the same could be said of Philemon and his household.

In other words, the core group consisted of multiple individuals to carry the load. I've seen many couples start house churches by themselves, surrounding themselves with those hurting and broken by life and are soon overwhelmed. One couple whose hearts are as big as the Grand Canyon in compassion, are always bringing people from very rough backgrounds to the Lord, but their efforts at starting a house church thus far have been in vain. Why? It is because they are trying to do it by themselves, when in fact they need some stability in their own lives. Though they have big hearts, they have very little parenting skills of their own children, and so aren't stable at home and unable to be part of a core in a house church. In fact, no one wants to join with them in sharing the responsibility of hosting and leading a house church because their lives and children lack basic discipline and manners.

Another couple started with a house church and seemed to be 'core' people, people of peace. Yet when their children played in the backyard of one of the host homes they wreaked havoc by breaking decorative stones around the water garden and throwing those stones at the fish, trying to kill them. They also tossed sticks and other debris into the swimming pool. When asked repeatedly to stop this behavior over the course of 3 weeks to no avail, the hosts went to the parents, who were immediately offended and left the house church. Their immaturity and offense revealed them as not being the mature ones Paul sought in I Timothy 3 or in other words, they weren't people of peace.

The biggest frustration as a leader is when you see the call of God on a person or a couple's life, but they refuse to enter into it. I've known several who are so caught up in their own lives they have no room for the commitment of (house) church. Preferring to drift between traditional churches with no pressure or responsibility expected of them, they are potential people of peace who have turned inwardly to their own selfishness, and as such have disqualified themselves, backing away from God's higher purpose in their lives.

When you link up with someone to start a house church, make sure that they really are capable of sharing the load and are on about the same maturity level and preferably roughly the same season of life as yourself...or older in the Lord and have already been where you are.

How does leadership arise?

Have you ever wondered how Paul could "appoint elders in every church" (Acts 14:23) when those churches were brand new and he barely knew them? As already stated, the 'elders' were people Paul noted had a natural care for their own spirituality and the care of those around them. The elders were people of peace who naturally rose to the surface and immediately became evident with only a little time together.

Paul made the point of getting to know people by their spirit, by their giftings in the Lord. II Corinthians 5:16:

"Henceforth know we no man after the flesh" (KJV)

"Consequently, from now on we estimate and regard no one from a (purely) human point of view..." (AMP)

Remember that the ekklesia is guided by divine revelation from the Father, and upon that Rock of revelation the ekklesia meets. Paul sought to know people by their spirit, their call in God, and by what the Holy Spirit was revealing to Paul about the Father's plan for their lives. He wasn't impressed by their resume' or life experience, he searched his spirit for revelation from the Father about His purpose for bringing these people across his path.

There are people you meet in life that you know immediately there is a divine connection. By the same token there are some you meet and it's just dead inside. Nice meeting you, but you can tell God has nothing more in store for the relationship. Paul is saying he was being sensitive to those divine connections the Father brought across his path.

This means that you will know by the Spirit who is to join you, who is the person(s) of peace, who God has called to be with you in the establishment of the (house) church. Look for a witness in the spirit man, that good feeling, that peace that indicates the Father leading by revelation. You can be sure that if it is the Father they too will have that revelation, for the Father does things in the mouth of more than one witness that every word may be confirmed.

In our network we do not use titles other than referring to people as leaders or hosts, but many of us could identify who the elders/pastors are in each house church because that gift comes to the forefront. It isn't a matter of trying to do something, the gifts and functions God has placed in the body just naturally flow.

In practice those who are gifted and function as elders/pastors often melt into the background once a meeting starts. If they aren't in charge of that meeting you may not even know that quiet person on the sofa is considered to be the main leader, because their heart is so to empower others and let God be God.

Paid staff?

We've found that a house church starts losing the dynamics if it gets above about 12–15 people. For brief periods we've risen to 20 or even 30 in a house church, but not for long. Soon there will be talk of breaking off into other house churches, and again we usually like 2–3 couples or at least 4–6 individuals to do so, that the burden not be on any one person's shoulders. Again, Lydia had a whole houseful of servants to help share the load, not to mention the jailer and his household. Tyrannus had a school and presumably staff, Philemon household servants, and so forth. Beyond that there was a bit of travel 'from house to house' as well.

One of our house churches was made up of a mix of 'empty nest' couples as well as several singles, and some who attended alone because a spouse didn't attend our church—trouble soon arose. I got a call that the singles weren't happy because they didn't feel the discussions were going toward subjects relevant to them, but instead revolved around marriage.

My mind immediately went to the 'church split' mentality of the traditional church. Whose feathers were ruffled? Who was in strife? But just as quickly my mind switched to New Testament mentality. If there were troubles it was because someone's needs were not being met. I knew each of the people involved and all of the single people qualified as people of peace, so I met with 4 of them and pointed out the need for another church, so that is exactly what they did. They divided out of the first church and started their own, rotating between their homes each week. Problem solved!

However, once a house church begins dividing out into 2 or more house churches, there may be a need to have someone who functions as an elder/pastor to be paid because the needs of the people may become a part or full time position. Paul addressed the need for this when he wrote to Timothy whom he had sent to Ephesus to help with leadership issues there. He said in I Timothy 5:17–18:

"Let the elders that rule well be counted worthy of double honor, especially they who labor in the word and doctrine. For the scripture says 'Thou shall not muzzle the ox that treads out the corn.' And 'The laborer is worthy of his reward.' (KJV)

The double honor is clearly that leaders may be paid, thus the references to muzzling the ox and the laborer being worthy of his wages. There is a stream in house church that doesn't believe in paid house church leadership, yet scripture can't be denied. Sometimes the issue is kept quiet and sometimes it's an out and out policy to never have someone paid 'over them' again. In each case I've seen this attitude and practice come from either hurt in the pyramid structure previously or a lack of understanding of a balanced, scriptural view of house church finances, or both.

Often Paul's experience of tent making in Corinth is mentioned in this regard which is valid for the 18 months he spent in that city in Acts 18, but what about the other 30 years of his ministry? Paul makes the case quite strongly for himself and the general principle of receiving offerings for his living in I Corinthians 9 and in the passage quoted above.

The means and methods of receiving tithes and offerings is discussed later, but the reader should not shy away from this possibility just because of a bad experience in the pyramid system.

One couple left a house church I know because the leader mentioned one little thing about offerings. When asked about why they left the husband acknowledged they had previously attended a church that pushed very hard on tithing and they were still hurt and overly sensitive to the subject of money. I would offer that the proof of a real $20 bill is the existence of a counterfeit. In many traditional churches the emphasis on money is so pervasive that many people have never experienced the true, Biblical practice of giving and receiving. House church is the opportunity to experience the True in this area.

For many pastors wanting to transition to house church from the pyramid this is the scariest part of the whole thing. How do I make the transition without going bankrupt? If we sell the building how do we make the transition? Will the people still give if there is no building to support? The answer is to follow the scriptural model of establishing people of peace serving in support of (house) churches with a means by which to receive tithes and offerings from the people.

When we first started in Tulsa and suddenly had 4 house churches going at the same time, I rotated to a different house church each week, sometimes sharing when I was there, sometimes not, and my wife and I were in the rotation for hosting as well. Even then it was a full time job helping the house church core leaders manage everyone and everything going on. It is even more needed now with a multi-state multi-national network.

Suffice to say that just like any other issue involving house church, the whole of the New Testament was written to people in house church and about their issues and situations. There is a scriptural way of developing leaders, paid and otherwise in the New Testament and just because many of us have experienced the bad part of these issues in the pyramid does not mean we should shy away from the True examples found in scripture. In fact we should run towards them, eager for the first time in our Christian lives to be living in and flowing in a fully scriptural church life.

Caring for one another's physical needs

This element illustrates one of the biggest differences between the traditional pyramid and the house church.

Many of us have sat in a traditional church and put money into the offering bucket while we think to ourselves about a person we know who is struggling financially. In the pyramid the money goes from the pew to the pastor and little if any is returned back to the people in the pews.

Not only is it unusual for a person to receive financial help from their church in pyramid structured churches, but if someone gives another person some money directly to them it is noted as an exception and worthy of a testimony on Wednesday night! This is because all focus is on the Moses at the top, the building program or other need, and not on looking around you in the pew to see who you can bless with a financial gift.

In the pyramid there is only what I call vertical giving. This means a person only gives upwards to the Moses at the top and there is no provision for giving horizontally to the person next to them in the pew. The giving goes to support the 4 walls of the pyramid (purpose, policies, direction, vision) rather than to the support of the base, its people.

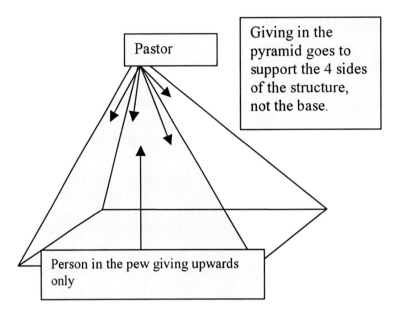

By contrast we see Acts 2:44–45

"And all that believed were together and had all things common; and sold their possessions and goods and parted them to all men, as every man had need." (KJV)

Acts 4:32, 34–35

"And the multitude of them that believed were of one heart and of one soul: neither said any of them that anything of the things which he possessed was his own, but they had all things common. Neither was there any among them that lacked: for as many as were possessors of lands or houses sold the, and brought the prices of the things that were sold, And laid them down at the apostles' feet: and distribution was made unto every man according as he had need." (KJV)

I've often made the comment that prosperity preachers would be laughed out of town if they could go back to the early church because the people in the first 300 years of Christianity gave everything to one another. If one had two coats he gave to him who had none. In our own network of house churches we've added a deck on a house, rebuilt engines, given cars, fixed cars, paid mortgages, bought food, paid utility bills, put tires on cars, and the list goes on. Why think of giving as being only in the realm of money? You are free to give anything and everything as you have and as needs arise, or help coordinate the meeting of needs with others.

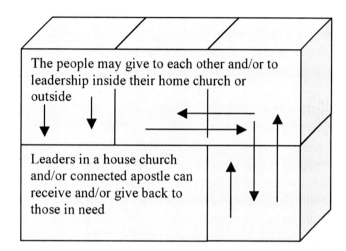

Remembering that Acts 8:1 tells us all the people (except the apostles) left town due to the persecution of Saul we understand through Paul's writings that giving among and between the house churches took on a new dimension once they left Jerusalem.

Acts 11:29–30 tells us that because of a prophetic word the church at Antioch gave money **'every man according to his ability'** to the saints in Judea. It wasn't specified to go to the leaders; the text says it went to the saints (which could include leaders of course).

In I Corinthians 16:1–2 Paul tells them that, along with the churches of Galatia, he will pick up the Corinthian's offering for the saints in Jerusalem as he passes through. He tells everyone to give **"as God has prospered him"**.

In II Corinthians 8 Paul boasts in the giving of the churches in Macedonia (the area of Philippi) and urges the Corinthians to **'abound in this grace also'** (8:7). We also see once again that giving is **"according to what a man has"** (8:12) (all KJV)

In Philippians 4:16, writing back to Lydia and the churches in Philippi, Paul thanks them for giving to him: **"For even in Thessalonica you sent once and again to meet my needs."** (KJV)

In house church there is the freedom for each person to decide between him or herself and the Lord on how to give, but there should be something in place in each house church to give both horizontally to each other, and to leadership. My experience has been that there is a considerable lag time between people freed from the pyramid's constant pressure and condemnation concerning giving and the time they decide in and of themselves to give on a regular basis. As Paul noted in I Corinthians 16:2:

"Upon the first day of the week let <u>every one of you</u> lay by him in store as God has prospered him..." (KJV)

This indicates that giving to others was a part of normal Christianity in Paul's time. But in our day it often takes some time before people start thinking in terms of setting aside something each paycheck for someone else. I've encouraged people to set a percentage, be it 3% or 5% to start to develop the discipline to set something aside for others within the house church and beyond each pay day plus be open to the Lord's prompting outside that set percentage. Yet I've found that those who tithed and gave in the pyramid continue to tithe and even increase their giving in house church.

It really is quite interesting to listen to a young couple go on and on about the great time at dinner and movie they had last week, only to have them say they don't have any money to give to the person needing help with their mortgage or to the leadership of the house church or network. As Paul wished, that you might abound in this grace also...

I am not dispensing legal advice, however most any accountant that specializes in clergy and ministry accounts will tell you that a church need not be incorporated nor have IRS 501(c)(3) status for member's giving to be tax deductible. In fact, one such company who has as some of their clients among the biggest names in church circles told me that in days past incorporating meant protection for the officers and pastor from lawsuits, but since Enron and other high profile cases in which the authorities and individuals went after the officers personally, incorporating for churches has little value for that purpose.

Many house churches that aren't set up as a regular church or ministry first can go to irs.gov and get an Employer Identification Number (EIN) and with that may open a bank account as a church. Once that is established a means of giving and receiving can be established among the leadership.

In our network we provide affiliates with a preaddressed envelope for those who wish to include myself and our network in their giving, but we also encourage a similar means to be able to give on a local level as well, though we have as a network sent money to members within our network as well. Because incorporating as a church may not be an option for many house churches, we cover our affiliates with a liability insurance package in three areas: Sexual misconduct, injury, and 'bad counsel'. We chose this because of the true experience of someone in a house church who injured their ankle while at someone's house during a house church meeting. When the homeowner filed a claim with his insurance company for reimbursement for the emergency room bill, he mentioned they were having church when the accident happened. The homeowner's insurance company then backed away saying that since it was a church meeting the church's policy should cover it. They had no such policy and so were out that money.

Elements of a balanced house church

In the early days of the home schooling movement some of the parents home schooled in a sort of haphazard 'we'll try it out' way. **They knew more about what they didn't want than what they did want.**

Such is the case with many people considering house church in the west today. Yet the answers which define a balanced house church are right there in Acts and the other letters of the New Testament. From them we can glean common elements that contributed to their overall balance and the health of the local house church.

These 9 elements are seen in the house churches of the New Testament: Evangelism, the teaching of the Word, prayer, worship, fellowship, corporate fellowship, caring for each other's needs, traveling/hosting, and being networked with other house churches via an apostle.

These should not be thought of as a pyramid structure like a program to be developed for the group to do. It's all relationship based and flows naturally from the giftings within the members, developing at a natural pace over time.

Evangelism and the teaching of the Word go hand in hand. As noted throughout this book, the house churches of the Bible were outwardly focused rather than inward, and their number one priority was furthering the discipleship process through the teaching of the Word of God. The vitality of their life in Christ flowed naturally outward to those in their spheres of influence, and others were brought in as a result.

To say they were involved in prayer and worship is to state the obvious. From the 120 praying in the upper room on Pentecost to praying in Mark's mom's house when Peter was in prison to the five men in Acts 13:1–3 praying for direction, prayer and worship was a large part of the life of the early church.

Today in house church, prayer does not revolve around those in the "office of intercessor" (there is no such thing), but involves anyone so inclined, though we acknowledge there are some graced and gifted as intercessors. That means there may or may not be set times of prayer during church or at other times, based on the gifts in any given house church, but there will be prayer for one another, the nation and issues and events in the world will be lifted up, but not as a program or separated group necessarily, but naturally flowing from its members.

There were two types of fellowship seen in the early church; fellowship within the house church, and fellowship with others in a larger corporate setting. Acts 2: 42:

"And they continued steadfastly...in fellowship and in breaking of bread..."

In other words, they fellowshipped among themselves in each local house church, but they did not stay an island to themselves; they also went house to house and were connected to what other believers were doing in their community..

They also came out of their houses to meet in larger settings, meeting members of other house churches, from other neighborhoods. This was also employed when decisions which affected the whole body needed to be made in Jerusalem, for in Acts 6: 2 we see the apostles calling **'the multitude of the disciples unto them'** when they needed to appoint deacons for the food service ministry. Prior to that, when Peter and John were released from prison it seems to have been a corporate meeting, as shown in Acts 4:23–32:

"And being let go, they went to their own group...they lifted up their voice to God with one accord...and when they had prayed the place was shaken...and the multitude of them that believed were of one heart and of one soul..." (KJV)

I observed that some doing house church insist that house church is the only way to do church, and often that means they won't set foot in a traditional pyramid style church. But there is great value in going to hear a speaker or a teacher in a traditional church or for the corporate worship or other purpose from time to time. After all, 3,000 people were gathered to hear Peter at Pentecost!

The difficulty is that the traditional church is focused on and often offers only, the corporate style of meeting. The facts that Jesus fed 5,000 and in another instance 4,000 men plus women and children illustrates the good in a corporate meeting; but those are the only two instances in 3 1/2 years of ministry that record huge crowds like that. Matthew even records that his Sermon on the Mount began as a private discourse to his disciples and only at the end did the people find him tucked away in the mountains (Mt 5:1; 7:28; 8:1) And as great as Pentecost was, there is no other large meeting like that recorded in the ensuing 30 years that Acts covers. Everything else was done in homes and among small numbers of people gathered.

Some would like to compare house church to cell church, confusing the two, but they are completely opposite. The cell is part of the larger pyramid, still focused on the corporate meeting as the primary meeting. In house church the small group **is** the meeting with random or planned meetings with others in the larger body of Christ in a community.

Healthy balanced house churches remain connected to the larger body of Christ in their community no matter the structure those churches utilize. A couple leaders in our network also attend ministerial alliance meetings on a regular basis in their communities. One leader told me when I had asked how he was accepted, "It took about a year, but now they understand and accept me."

It is healthy to be involved with what God is doing in your city or town. I think sometimes people in house churches are hesitant to become involved with city wide prayer meetings or other events because the concept of the house church is still a foreign language to many. When they ask 'What church do you belong to?' or 'What churches do we have represented here today?' some feel inadequate and put on the spot to say, 'I belong to a house church'. It was the same way in the 1980s when we said we home schooled our children. People either scurried away quickly avoiding us like the plague or were at the place that they asked questions. So it is in house church today. Oddly enough, it is often the unbeliever who says 'that's the way church should be done', while the traditional church person runs the other way as fast as possible!

I observed that many house churches that don't have members who meet with others outside of themselves often lack identity and purpose. They can also get off doctrinally. I mentioned earlier a group that got off into the inner healing teaching exclusively. In one city I was told that house churches 'start and shut down, start and shut down'. My experience in that city is a lack of leadership, identity, and connection, and the house church I attended while there was focused completely on hurt suffered in the traditional church. I was told that was the norm. Without fellowshipping with others it's very easy to get a defensive, even cynical view of 'the church'. Conversations in house church meetings that are focused inward can take on a tone of 'us versus them' and I've seen an arrogance that has crept into some house churches with the mindset that 'we have the answers.'

Remember that God flows to the fullest amount he can through whatever structure man gives him, and we should accept those 'streams', for as Paul said in another context, they do it unto the Lord—God accepts them, so we should too. Fellowshipping with others in the body, no matter what stream they are in, opens our eyes to what God is doing in the larger picture. It keeps us balanced.

I observed that often the people who refuse to fellowship corporately with the larger body of Christ are still dealing with hurts and issues within themselves, making external excuses about why they can't or won't come to the larger fellowship.

The house churches that are islands to themselves are just as far on that end of the pendulum as the traditional church pastor who refuses to let his members go to any other church or service.

The last 2 elements are traveling/hosting and being connected to a network via an apostle. It seemed Paul was having a continual exchange of people going back and forth within his network of house churches.

Paul was always sending or receiving people such as Timothy, Silas, Titus, Phoebe, Epaphras (Col 1:7), Tychicus (Col 4:7), Luke, Demas, Mark, Trophimus (II Tim 4:20), and others. As we read the New Testament we gather that at any given time an untold number of people were traveling between house churches all over the Roman Empire.

I think it's a quality that is quite unlike anything in the pyramid structure. In the pyramid the people at the bottom are free to go to any church or meeting or convention they wish, but those meetings are usually held in the auditorium of a (pyramid) traditional church, thus it's a bunch of strangers meeting to hear one speaker or topic. Also in the pyramid the main exchange is when a guest speaker comes in or the pastor leaves and someone fills in for him while he is gone. The New Testament presents dozens of people traveling to one another's homes in a sort of continual exchange and fellowship.

Within the New Testament the opening of homes to travelers and the sending of people to others in house church circles is basic and very healthy. Affirmation of each other and the sharing of ideas and talking through problems enriches everyone. The fact that we can see in the Bible 'chapter and verse' these travels and hosting elements should not be a surprise, though it is often overlooked.

III John 5–8 talks about faithfully serving travelers, saying '**we ought to receive such, that we might be fellow helpers to the truth**'. (v8—KJV)

Nearly everyone remembers Hebrews 13:2 and the exhortation to '**receive travelers, for some have entertained angels unawares.'** (KJV)

They weren't traveling just for travel's sake. They were seeking relationships, wanting to know 'how they are doing', wanting to meet and encourage others of like precious faith. Paul said in Acts 15:36 to Barnabas:

"Let us go again and visit our brethren in every city where we have preached the Word of the Lord, and see how they do." (KJV)

This is travel with purpose, direction, and impartation intended and it often involves visiting different cultures, such as when the Jewish leaders from Jerusalem visited the Gentile believers in Antioch (Gal 2:11–14). Keep in mind as well that when they traveled it was often to different countries. Israel, Turkey, and Greece are all mentioned. Additionally people coming or going to Libya, Cyprus, Niger, Spain, Yugoslavia and others are mentioned. As the Lord seeks to fill the earth with himself by filling every ethnic group, we must travel to see the larger picture of God's personality as demonstrated in those cultures.

Another reason this is good is because it turns the eyes outward to the bigger picture of world evangelism. Look at the book of Acts and Paul's letters. They are more than just the history of how the church grew; they show that they grew in part due to people traveling back and forth, sharing ideas, revelation, and concepts, being mutually enriched in Christ as a result.

With the church being based in the home, it is natural to host people in that home. I'm not suggesting everyone has to open their home, motels are just fine. But there are people who have gifts of hospitality and are truly anointed to do so or folks who just have the room and enjoy hosting. So I'm not saying everyone has to host someone, just that hosting and traveling are a good part of a balanced house church. The 'real' atmosphere of staying with people during a visit automatically brings down walls, provides a chance to learn from each other, and then in turn those experiences are brought back to 'home' base.

It appears in the New Testament that (concerning travel) there were three groups of people. The first group represents those that have no desire to travel to other house churches or cultures. They can be seen in Acts 20:17 when Paul called for a meeting with the leaders of the churches in Ephesus. They were concerned about their community and had no desire to travel outside. This can be seen in part during Paul's departure where he told them they would never see him again. If they had been willing to travel to Rome, where he was going, they could have visited him there, for Acts closes with Paul spending two years in his own rented home in Rome. Their heart though was at home and with their own people.

The second group involves those interested in the local body, but they also want to travel. The names mentioned above would be included in this group. It seems Aquilla and Priscilla moved around a bit for they are mentioned in several places, but Paul always sends greetings 'to the church in your house'. They had a heart and call to the local body, but also traveled. Timothy and Titus are two others that come to mind, the former being sent to Ephesus and the later to Crete.

In modern times this would be the person willing to travel to different house churches within a country or to other countries for short term trips. Not everyone in a house church will want to travel; some will be like the first group, just concerned about their local church, which is fine. Perceive the grace in each other and help each other live out what God has placed in their hearts.

The third group would be full time ministers like Paul and other apostles. They traveled all over, settling down for a season, but after awhile moving on. He was a year in Antioch, 1 1/2 to 2 years in Corinth, over two years in Ephesus, two years in Rome, and so on…settling until the Lord moved him on.

The last element found in the New Testament that is perhaps the most difficult for those burned by the pyramid to accept, and that is that every (house) church in the New Testament was part of and connected to apostles.

The apostles tied together the far ranging house churches by visiting, writing letters, sending associates to help local churches, and so on. We can understand this tying together simply by looking at the whole of the New Testament. From Matthew's gospel to The Revelation, apostles or those closely associated with apostles wrote these letters. Their effect was the balancing out of doctrine and the cementing of relationships as these young churches multiplied across the Roman Empire.

Yet in our day there has been such abuse of the gift of 'sent ones' that even if one accepts the premise that house churches are for today, the idea of being connected to an apostle gives one pause.

If not known for abuse, then certainly most who call themselves apostles sit atop a pyramid structure, requiring apt attention from subordinates and perhaps even tithing directly to them (something Paul never required or even suggested).

Our minds automatically click over to pyramid mode, since that is where most of us first learned of apostles, and as a result many house churches run from any talk of being connected to an apostle or part of a larger network, but again this is because they are hearing the words 'apostle' or 'network' through the eyes of a bad experience in the pyramid church.

For quite some time I looked at the differences between people who meet in a home and call it a house church, and those whose house churches were either started by or connected with, balanced apostolic leaders. There is a marked difference in the previous 8 elements listed above, if they are present at all in house churches without apostolic leadership.

There is a basic anointing that exists when people get together in the name of the Lord for fellowship, the Word and so forth. But there is another anointing that seems to pervade the very atmosphere of a house church with purpose and God's presence when that house church has apostolic leadership.

I don't care for the term 'covering', as that is clearly a pyramid term. Perhaps viewing apostles as foundations provides a more accurate picture depicting a local house church standing and built upon a firm foundation. That foundation is an ongoing relationship with a balanced apostle.

One of the greatest gifts of an apostle that I see in scripture through Paul's visits and letters back to the churches is that of just talking through the process of church and discipleship with people. Apostles travel to develop relationships and by sitting down with people and just talking through issues. That is not direction from above, but rather as part of the foundation helping to build the Living Temple from beneath and from within by just talking it through.

As Paul told the church in I Corinthians 1:24:

"Not for that we have dominion over your faith, but are helpers of your joy: for by faith you stand." (KJV)

Do apostles always start the churches they guide?

No. Consider the facts presented in scripture: The churches in Acts were started by apostles, an evangelist (Philip, Acts 8), or just by people spreading the word and meeting together like Antioch in Acts 11:19. However, each and every church in the New Testament soon became associated with apostles after they started. The precedent set forth in Acts shows that churches can start without apostles initiating it, but then they linked up with the apostles soon after. Philip turned the new believers over to apostles Peter and John once he was going to leave the area.

I hesitate even writing about 'apostolic' leadership because the reader may still be filtering what is written through life experience in the pyramid rather than the scripture put forth here. Let the reader understand I am not talking to, or leading up to a power trip pyramid structure. I'm just making observations from scripture and what the Holy Spirit continues to do around the world today. Genuine apostles can be found at the bottom of the Living Temple, serving from the bottom up, cognizant of their authority, but tempered with humility. Just talking through the process with the people they serve seems to be the primary means of guiding the development of house based churches.

Based on the facts set forth in scripture, that the only examples we have of church planting in the Bible show that it is done by apostles or close associates and becomes linked with apostles, we should be confident that this is the method God has ordained. Think of it; Romans, Corinthians, Galatians, Ephesians, Philippians, Colossians, Thessalonica…all started by apostles. Beyond these regions and cities there was Antioch, Cyprus, Crete, Iconium, Lystra, Sardis, Thyatira and so on who were related to the apostles. They all networked together, traveled and hosted back and forth, passing Paul and Peter's letters among themselves, and copying the same so more could learn. They were connected to apostles no matter how they got started.

Again, this wasn't top down leadership, but from the bottom up. In corporate America there are franchises. Each franchise has a local owner, or set of owners who are responsible for the oversight of their business. They have a corporate umbrella that helps maintain order and a degree of uniformity, but corporate doesn't tell the local franchise what to do unless it violates published policy, ethics, morals, or the law.

If house church is the franchise with each office independently 'owned and operated', then the traditional church is IBM. If house church is like a collection of stores in an open air mall all interdependent upon each other for survival, then traditional church is a warehouse store with everything under one roof.

In Satan's imitation of the house church, is it any wonder he puts forth a counterfeit at the same time the legitimate is expanding rapidly; that is the terrorist networks. These imitations of the True bring death and destruction to many, yet are independently run, receiving only guidance, advice, and strategy from 'corporate' so to speak. You may not have thought of terror networks as Satan's house church, but in principle it's true. They are the counterfeits. They meet with purpose, are committed to each other, and claim divine revelation to do what they do.

True apostles are then the spiritual fathers, the teachers, the mentors offering guidance, not demanding obedience. Apostles come alongside to help, first in authority, yet also first in service balanced by love.

Revelation is what the Kingdom is based on, and apostles bring it fresh from the Cornerstone. They survey the rest of the building and have a greater revelation of the whole structure, even as Paul wrote most of the New Testament based on his revelations. He said he was a co-worker with God and claimed to be a wise master-builder (I Cor 3:9–10), but this lofty claim is balanced by his previous acknowledgment that though one may water and another may plant, those are nothing, only God who gives the increase gets the glory. In Romans 1:11 he says he wants to impart to them some spiritual gift. The word 'impart' means to give a share of, not giving away, but sharing what he has.

Apostles that are truly apostles are ones a house church would want to be connected with. They are not corporate coming down from above controlling everything, but more like overseeing (under-seeing) a franchise as one who has worked from the bottom up, offering help and guidance as needed, but leaving the 'franchise' to stand on it's own two feet.

All the churches in the New Testament were started by apostles or linked with apostles and there is no other example in scripture for us to follow. Therefore there is a marked difference between people just 'meeting together' to have a house church, and those who are linked with an apostle.

How can I further illustrate the difference? I believe chapters two & three of the book of The Revelation demonstrate this difference: The Lord sends a message 'to the angel of the church at' in each of the seven churches mentioned, indicating that they are the 'behind the scenes' spiritual authority assigned to the church for protection.

Some might suggest the word 'angel' is a man, for in the pyramid structured churches we came out of some teach it was 'the' pastor, ignoring the fact that the first century churches weren't ruled by 1 pastor, thus disqualifying that theory. So this argument falls by the way side quickly.

My point is that there are angels over all these churches, indicating the Divine Purpose for the existence of that church, and all of them were of course, started by apostles or linked with apostles. I believe the angelic covering, which shows the Lord ordained these churches and watches over them, is the difference between people just meeting and calling themselves a house church, and a house church started by or linked relationally with apostles.

Most everyone who reads this can remember a time when they walked into a church building or meeting and even though the Word may have come forth, there was an overriding sense of 'deadness' in the spiritual atmosphere. Others may have watched a church split and one group head off to start a church, but it only lasted a short time. It just didn't 'feel' right. What you sensed was that there was no angelic covering ordaining the existence of that church. It should be stated that the angelic covering is an indicator that the Lord Himself has ordained that church to be there.

The first church I ever pastored in the pyramid structure in about 1981 had no covering anointing. I wondered why, though the Word was anointed, it seemed to fall to the ground when I taught. The same 6 families that had hired me to be their pastor were the only ones to stay at that church. Finally, after about 6 months or so of this, I spent some time in prayer and lightly fasting to find out why. On the third day the Lord told me: "I never ordained this church to be started. I want you to shut it down and tell them I have churches for them to go to."

It turned out they were a group of Baptists who had become Charismatic and were tired of their pastor wavering between 'yes' on tongues and 'no' on tongues, so they started meeting on their own in a trailer park club house. I told them what the Lord told me and we did shut it down. We remained on good terms with those people for many years, though since then we've lost track of one another.

Though there were believers gathered together to have church there was no anointing from God for that effort. There was just something missing. That something was the angelic, God ordained purpose and covering for the church. The key is that they had no divine Revelation that they were to be a church. They just started meeting after being fed up with the pastor. They had the commitment and purpose, but there was no divine revelation concerning them being a church.

Perhaps some reading this can relate to house churches or pyramid style churches that seem OK, but something is missing. What Christians automatically look for, even on a subconscious level, is something in their spirit that says God has ordained this group. On many occasions there is no covering anointing and that is why people don't feel the presence of the Lord in that place. I'm not trying to over-simplify everything, but only offer an answer why some house churches seem to be ordained by God and others just seem to be a bunch of good hearted people meeting together.

Apostolic leadership in action

The truth is that Jesus told his apostles to submit to those they serve. Mark 10: 42–44 makes this quite clear, so the idea of a power hungry 'apostle' just does not exist. Apostles are servants, teachable, content to wait their turn, eager to impart, and quietly confident in their purpose and destiny. My observation has been that if an apostle is 'power hungry' he sits on top a pyramid.

In II Corinthians 10:13–16 Paul says this:

"We, on the other hand, will not boast beyond our legitimate province and proper limit, but will keep within the limits (or our commission which) God has allotted us as our measuring line, and which reaches and includes even you. For we are not overstepping the limits of our province and stretching beyond our ability to reach...We do not boast therefore beyond our proper limit over other men's labors...without making a boast of work already done in another (man's) sphere of activity (before we came on the scene)..." (AMP)

Paul is only concerned with what God gave him. He is not competitive and is very much aware that others have contributed to the building of this church. Such is the humility of an apostle as set forth in scripture. Paul wanted to work his field and not another man's, and when done he wanted to move to another set of people

God had assigned him to. He and/or his team of travelers would move on to the next door God opened.

I have also observed that raising up leaders is often a shortcoming of some house churches. John Maxwell says of leadership, that on a scale of 1 to 10, if you are a 5, the people you oversee can never rise beyond a 4. Jesus said the student isn't greater than his teacher. One of the solutions for this is the 'new life' that comes through traveling and outside contact, raising everyone to greater maturity.

If an up and coming leader isn't exposed to leadership outside their circle, they will never rise to the place of being able to replace that leadership if the need arises, or be able to plant new churches as the Lord leads. Contact with the larger body of Christ also helps speak into lives that might otherwise insulate themselves from other forms of 'doing church'.

The process seems to follow the way Paul imparted to Timothy. Timothy traveled with Paul, learning about God and the ministry, and then Paul sent him to Ephesus for some 'you're on your own' application. It was a successful method; Foxes Book of Martyrs records that Timothy stayed in Ephesus some 30 years, becoming elder/bishop over the area until he was killed for his faith in the year 97.

Without the 9 elements seen in scripture first founded upon Revelation, Purpose and Commitment to each other, there is no heart in a house church to link with others in the body of Christ, there is no desire to win others to the Lord and raise up people who will reach out and plant other churches. They may become dangerously out of balance in other areas as well.

As Peter mentioned the character traits to add to our faith, and then summarized by saying 'if these are in you and abound, they will make you so that you will not be barren nor unfruitful', and we constantly jostle with those qualities as we grow in the Lord; so will a house church jostle around a bit as these qualities mix together. House church is a living, breathing organism seeking the Lord's best in each other while making allowances for one another, trying to keep the unity of the faith by love.

The whole kingdom operates on revelation, and that is a process with many layers. This is a normal part of the maturing process that I noticed within myself. I was seeking something more than the traditionally structured church could offer, but wanted to keep my heart right in all areas.

The journey of seeking God outside the structure of the traditional church began with what I thought was just me, a spiritual dissatisfaction, wanting more of God. The journey took me however from the temple mentality to the correct New Testament understanding that Christ lives in me, a living temple of God.

I searched the Word and what God was doing in the world, and concluded that the highest and best way to 'do church' is church as an extension of family, friends and community, in short, the house based church. I left the church to become the church, not disgruntled and with a bad attitude, but rather seeking a place where God was in charge of the agenda through his people, and I was seeking closer relationships with people on the same spiritual page.

In the process I discovered my own gifts and that spiritual satisfaction does not come by seeking the spectacular, but rather through ordinary day-in, day-out relationships in all their struggles and glory.

Epilogue

How "The Church Without Walls International of Tulsa" came into being

The seeds of CWOWI were planted in 1992. During a time of prayer the Lord Jesus appeared to me in a visitation and shared some of what he was going to be doing in the future. Part of what he said included a bit of a history lesson. He said that during the Charismatic renewal of the 1960's and 70's many people came out of the traditional churches because their needs were not being met and they were hungry for the deeper things of God.

As a result, many 'para-church' organizations were raised up and played an important role in the discipling of these new believers. (Two organizations that come to mind are Full Gospel Businessmen's International and Aglow) He told me that as a result of that 'exodus' teaching and evangelistic organizations soon started Bible schools to train and equip pastors and leaders.

The Lord then said that many of these pastors and churches that were raised up during that time have now become as "structured, rigid, and set on their own agendas as the churches they came from" and I would again see an exodus from them.

He went on to say that many of the 'new' churches were no longer meeting the needs of the people and the people were looking for "depth, relationships, a free flowing move of the Spirit, and leadership that does not play political games". He said that there would again be a move "of what you call para-church organizations", home prayer meetings, and also home based churches raised up.

Jesus shared how many of his people were not in fellowship anywhere or were dissatisfied where they were because of "hurt, misuse and abuse, politics, and leadership caught up in the things of the flesh." He also added some commentary saying "that many of my people are facing the choice of conforming to what is being presented or getting out, not willing to compromise what they know is right." That was 1992.

At the beginning of 2001 I was seeking the Lord as to what His next move would be. Having observed the 'hot' revival centers either cooling or getting spiritually off and not seeing anything on the horizon, this was a matter of prayer being kept on the 'front burner' before the Lord.

In February 2001 I was invited to conduct a seminar and minister at a church in Mississauga, Ontario, which is in the Toronto area. During the morning worship service my eyes were opened to the Spirit realm and I saw Jesus walk over to me saying in part:

"Do not look at the TV and larger media ministries to try to understand what I am doing in my body today. They have a part to play, but they are the visible-to-the-eye veneer of my body that people see. Those that are carnal and immature see the outward appearance and are impressed, thinking these are the height of ministry and where the Spirit is concentrating today. But they are mistaken."

"See what I see, many small churches and ministries investing in relationships, walking in love, pouring their lives into each other, this is where the Spirit is moving today. There is a revolution taking place in my body, a revolution of relationships and discipleship and love. This will affect whole communities and economies."

"See what I see, many churches all over the world in which people are accountable to one another, working through conflicts, walking in love and growing as my disciples. This where the Spirit is moving today."

"Many are running to and fro asking, 'Where is the next move, what is the next season of the Spirit?', and I say to you it is under their very noses. They stumble at the supernatural work in their midst and refuse to humble themselves and be taught, because they seek the sensational and that which appeals to the outward man. They fail to recognize the true move of God because it must be spiritually discerned."

He continued: "You will see this revolution continue to grow and even be recognized by many, but not as a fad or a 'flashy' move of the Spirit. The discerning will perceive in their spirits that this is an abiding move, as it has been from the beginning so it must be now, I am moving in relationships. This will be a time of separation within my body. This is the most important point I'm sharing with you today; the true disciples are losing their taste for the shallow and the carnal, and separating themselves from those caught up in the appearance of spirituality. These are my army, the ones no one knows, these are the ones I am raising up, not to be known of man, but to be known of God."

"You are part of this move. This move is not a move of the masses, but of the individual. Make disciples; teach the ways of the Spirit, for many are hungry to truly know me, and the Father. Lead them into intimacy and growth in Me. Hear what the Spirit is saying to the church."

The impact of that visitation stayed with me throughout the year and started me looking at the differences between what I saw in the Word versus what I saw in the church world. At various times during the year people would come across my path and say things that rang true in my spirit concerning how people in church should be treated, how church ought to be, or telling how they had been hurt by pastors and churches.

By the end of October 2001 I had come to the conclusion that the pattern established in the New Testament of small groups meeting in homes, empowering each other and the Holy Spirit to move and be moved, was the way the Lord intended. Clearly this order allowed people to develop the nurturing relationships Jesus spoke about in the visitation and demonstrated in his Word. Though not wanting to pastor a church again I told my wife that if we ever did, it would be in our living room connected to other home churches.

About 3 weeks later, on November 4, 2001, during an evening meeting in a church in Edmonton, Canada, Jesus appeared again to me. As the host pastor and I fell to our knees (the host pastor did not see Jesus, but could feel he was there, though 3 others saw him) Jesus laid hands on me and said: "You've been doing the work of an apostle, and now I am laying hands on you ordaining you as an apostle." He told me to start a home church network "based on my Word and the things you've learned through the people I've brought across your path this year." "Structure it in such a way to facilitate the development of house churches around the world."

I was really in disbelief, having had no intention of leaving what I was doing. I asked him if he had a name in mind and he said immediately, 'The Church Without Walls International.'

He told me to meet with leaders and those whose hearts he would touch and spend the rest of the year (2001) patterning a home church after what he had been teaching. He said he would control the growth of it and that after the first of the year (beginning 2002) 'you may start other home churches at your discretion'.

The Church Without Walls International began meeting in the Fenn home in January 2002 and is growing and gaining affiliate house churches at a pace appropriate as relationships develop.

To contact John or for more information visit our web site:
www.iFaithhome.org or interactivefaith.org
Or write to:
The Church Without Walls International (CWOWI)
PO Box 70
Mounds, OK 74047

Printed in the United States
73575LV00004BA/3-164